The Book of Revelation

The Book of Revelation

A Study Manual

by

CHARLES DE SANTO

BAKER BOOK HOUSE
Grand Rapids, Michigan

Library of Congress Catalog Card Number: 67-18174

Copyright 1967 by
Baker Book House Company

ISBN: 0-8010-2818-3

First printing, April 1967
Second printing, January 1970
Third printing, July 1972
Fourth printing, June 1974

PHOTOLITHOPRINTED BY CUSHING - MALLOY, INC.
ANN ARBOR, MICHIGAN, UNITED STATES OF AMERICA
1974

Dedicated to
my wife, Norma
and the children
Steve, Deb, Susie, and Tim

PREFACE

This commentary is designed for the serious Bible student. It is based upon the text of the Revised Standard Version, unless otherwise stated. Occasionally references are made to the original *Greek* text but these are relatively few in number. I have attempted to bring out the clear meaning of the text without undue reference to the Greek. It seemed more appropriate to leave the *utensils* of scholarship in the study, and write a commentary which, like the others in this series, actually conveys the message of the Apocalypse. For those who are interested in detailed exegetical study, several volumes are suggested in the bibliography, and there are many, many more.

Many of the exhaustive commentaries on the book of Revelation, and some not so exhaustive, have pointed to similarities between Johannine thought and imagery, and that found in other religions and cultures. While I realize the importance of backgrounds, I felt that such material was not within the scope of this series. Furthermore, I strongly believe that where there is similarity of thought imagery, the inspired Apostle thoroughly baptizes any material he appropriates into the Christian faith for his inspired purpose. What we have said of non-biblical material is also true of that from the Old Testament. Although John's Apocalypse is saturated with allusions from the Old Testament Scriptures, *yet* we must not force an Old Testament meaning into his use of it. We must let John's message convey the ideas he intended when he wrote. The important question is not where John got his material but what John, inspired by the Holy Spirit, is saying!

It is hoped that the student will read the actual text of the book of Revelation several times before he attempts to understand the message of the book. After he has read the Apocalypse, then in consultation with the commentary, the message will begin to become clear. The student will profit by looking up the numerous references which were included to shed light upon the text. Much can be learned by comparing "Scripture with Scripture."

I wish to express my gratitude to my colleague, Professor Arthur Gathman, for his careful reading of the manuscript, and to Mrs. Robert Earl Tippin for her technical suggestions and her careful typing of the manuscript.

May the Lord bless this commentary to the end that the Word of God in the Apocalypse may become clearer and more relevant to the reader's Christian witness.

CHARLES DE SANTO

Huntington College
Huntington, Indiana

BIBLIOGRAPHY

COMMENTARIES

Alford, H., *The Greek Testament*, Vol. IV, Chicago: Moody Press, 1958 (revised by E. F. Harrison)

Barclay, W., *The Revelation of John*, Philadelphia: Westminster, Press, 1959 (The Daily Study Bible, 2 Vols.)

Beasley-Murray, G. R., "Revelation," in the *New Bible Commentary*, edited by F. Davidson, Grand Rapids: Eerdmans, 1953

Beckwith, I. T., *The Apocalypse of John*, New York: Macmillan, 1919. Reprinted Grand Rapids: Baker Book House, 1967

Charles, R. H., *A Critical and Exegetical Commentary on the Revelation of St. John*, Edinburgh: T. and T. Clark, 1920 ("The International Critical Commentary," Vols. 19, 20)

Erdman, C. R., *The Revelation of John*, Philadelphia: Westminster Press, 1936.

Love, J. P., *Revelation*, Richmond: John Knox Press, 1960 ("The Layman's Bible Commentary," Vol. 25)

Moffatt, J., *The Revelation of St. John the Divine*, Grand Rapids: Eerdmans, 1951 ("The Expositor's Greek Testament," Vol. 5)

Rist, M., *The Revelation of St. John the Divine*, New York: Abingdon Press, 1957 ("The Interpreter's Bible," Vol. XII)

Scott, C. Anderson, *Revelation*, London: Henry Frowde Publisher, n.d. ("The New-Century Bible")

Swete, H. B., *The Apocalypse of St. John*, New York: Macmillan, 1909

Turner, N., "Revelation," in *Peake's Commentary on the Bible*, revised by H. H. Rowley and M. Black, New York: Thomas Nelson & Sons, 1962

GENERAL INTRODUCTIONS

Guthrie, D., *New Testament Introduction*, (Hebrews to Revelation), Chicago: Inter-Varsity Press, 1964

Price, J. L., *Interpreting the New Testament*, New York: Holt, Rinehart, and Winston, 1961

Rist, M., "The Introduction," in the *Interpreter's Bible*, Vol. XII, New York: Abingdon Press, 1957

OUTLINE OF THE BOOK OF REVELATION

I. INTRODUCTION (1:1-3)
A. The Revelation (1:1a)
B. The Messenger (1:1b-2)
C. The Blessing (1:3)

II. A GENERAL LETTER TO THE SEVEN CHURCHES (1:4-20)
A. The Greeting (1:4-5a)
B. The Doxology (1:5b-6)
C. The Second Advent (1:7-8)
D. The Initial Vision (1:9-20)
   1. John on Patmos (1:9-11)
   2. The Son of Man Amid the Churches (1:12-20)
      a. His Character (1:12-15)
      b. His Ministry (1:16-17a)
      c. His Resources (1:17b-18)
   3. The Structure of the Book (1:19)

III. THE LETTERS TO THE SEVEN CHURCHES (2:1–3:22)
A. The Letter to the Church at Ephesus (2:1-7)
   1. The City of Ephesus
   2. The Commendation (2:2-3, 6)
   3. The Condemnation (2:4)
   4. The Call to Repentance (2:5)
   5. The Blessing (2:7)
B. The Letter to the Church at Smyrna (2:8-11)
   1. The City of Smyrna
   2. The Commendation (2:9-10b)
   3. The Blessing (2:10c-11)
C. The Letter to the Church at Pergamum (2:13-17)
   1. The City of Pergamum
   2. The Commendation (2:13)
   3. The Condemnation (2:14-15)
   4. The Call to Repentance (2:16)
   5. The Blessing (2:17)
D. The Letter to the Church at Thyatira (2:18-29)
   1. The City of Thyatira
   2. The Commendation (2:19)

11

INTRODUCTION

The last book in the Bible is by no means the least in importance. Rather it is the fitting climax of God's revelation of his will and purposes for the Christian and history. Whereas Genesis began by relating the story of the creation and Paradise lost, the Revelation concludes by showing how Paradise is regained and the new creation is ushered in.

The word "revelation" comes to us from the Latin. In the Greek the title of the book is "Apocalypse," which literally means "a disclosure." An apocalypse is a revelation or a disclosure of truth which heretofore has been unknown. In this "Apocalypse of John," God discloses his steadfast purpose to complete the redemption of his people and the world, which he inaugurated by the work of Christ during his first advent.

An apocalypse is a message of hope in times of despair. John is by no means the first prophet God has used to convey his message through the literary genre of apocalypse. There are apocalyptic sections in Isaiah, Ezekiel, Joel and Daniel. Even our Lord Jesus Christ used apocalyptic as a medium of expression (Mark 13). Let us look more closely at the characteristics of this tool which John used.

I. Characteristics of Apocalyptic Literature

A. An apocalypse is a "drama in two acts." The author is living in the midst of adverse circumstances from which he sees no means of escape except by divine intervention. This first act of the drama, therefore, is the "last days" of the evil age in which he finds himself, and the second act will be ushered in with the new creation.

B. Apocalyptic deals with the future, i.e., it is prophetic in nature, and yet it is different from prophetic books. A prophet was one who usually *spoke* his message. One of the primary concerns of the prophet is social morality, but the apocalyptic writer emphasizes impending judgment and deliverance. A prophet attempts to reform society, but the apocalyptist believes the present state is beyond remedy — only divine intervention can help.

C. Now there were many apocryphal apocalypses which were circulating in John's time. These may be seen in R. H. Charles' large volume *The Pseudepigrapha*, and in some of the

Qumran Scrolls (see *The Dead Sea Scrolls in English* by G. Vermes). But these non-canonical works are clearly inferior, their structure is not always orderly, and they are usually pseudonymous. John's work, on the other hand, is well organized and genuine.

Contrary to what some scholars have advocated, John is not to any appreciable degree dependent upon these apocryphal apocalypses, but rather his work is grounded in Old Testament prophetic literature. Aside from perhaps two allusions to I Enoch (Rev. 4:6; 6:11), John's allusions are all from the Old Testament: Daniel, Ezekiel, Zechariah, Isaiah, Jeremiah, Joel, Exodus, etc. Of the 404 verses in Revelation, only 126 contain no allusion to the Old Testament. But even though John was saturated with the Old Testament Scriptures, he was no mere "compiler" of Scripture verses. His work is an original revelation from God conveyed through Christ, to the angel, to John (Rev. 1:10). Whatever the Old Testament context from which he drew his material may have been, we should not try to fit Revelation into an Old Testament strait jacket. We must lay hold of the message Christ is conveying *through John*.

D. In order to understand Revelation, certain additional characteristics of apocalyptic literature should be kept in mind. Apocalyptic is symbolic. The images used are never meant to be literally drawn, but they are designed to convey a religious or spiritual truth. The reader must look beyond the image and the symbol to the intended truth. This is not to say that Revelation is not authentic. It is! Its truth, however, will be lost if a strict literalism is employed in interpretation. Figures, plus combinations of them, are all used by John to convey his messages of judgment and hope.

1. The numbers which occur most frequently are 3, 3½, 4, 5, 6, 7, 10, and 12:

Three — symbolizes the spirit world, either good or evil
Three and one-half — a cut-off or limited period of time
Four — the earth number
Five and ten — round numbers
Six — one short of the perfect number. It is the human number; a man is always short of perfection.
Seven — the perfect number; symbolizes completeness
Twelve — symbolizes God's redeemed people — Israel and the church
1000 and 144,000 — the first is the cube of ten and the lat-

ter, "the square of the Church number twelve, multiplied by the cube of the round number ten."

2. John also used figures of living creatures to symbolize various qualities:

the lion — strength. It is used to picture Christ the "Lion of the Tribe of Judah (Rev. 5:5; cf. I Peter 5:8).
the bear — stealth
the tiger — fierceness
the goat — evil
the ox or calf — patient service
the eagle — "high flight or spirituality"
the lamb — sacrifice
the face of man — intelligence

3. Perhaps we are more familiar with the colors used:

white — triumph and often purity
red — strife or war
black — famine
pale or greenish grey — death
green — eternal life
purple — royalty

4. When John wants to convey the reality of God's judgment, he uses a variety of natural portents and symbols:

cataclysms and convulsions — God's righteous judgment
earth — "seat of false religion"
sea — basis of false government

One might ask why God used this highly symbolic genre of apocalyptic to reveal his message. The answer which is usually given is that the apocalyptic symbolism could be understood by the church but not by the Romans. Thus John could safely communicate with his fellow believers.

II. How to Interpret the Apocalypse

Historically there have been four basic methods of interpreting the book of Revelation, each with something commendable about it. They are (1) preteristic, (2) historical, (3) futuristic, and (4) prophetic-apocalyptic.

A. The *preteristic* method relates to the past, i.e., John's own day. According to this interpretation, John was cryptically referring to the rise of Rome and its ruthless persecution of the church. The future references are understood as referring to the immediate future, i.e., shortly after John wrote. The Beast,

Babylon, the Harlot, etc., *only* symbolize Rome of the first century.

While it is true that John does write in the midst of a period of dire persecution in the early history of the church, it is a violation of the prophetic role to limit his message to the first century. A prophet, and this is what John calls himself (Rev. 22:9), speaks to his own day, but also to the future.

B. The *historical* interpreters attempt to pin-point events in history from the days of the Roman Empire to the end-time to which they believe John is alluding. Often the messages to the seven churches are made to apply to successive ages, the Laodicean age being the last. Unfortunately, this interpretation has attempted to do what Christ said he could not do — relate the *precise time* of the end. Historicists have interpreted the number 666 to refer to popes, dictators, and even Martin Luther. Certainly no Christian doubts the applicability of the prophetic message to every age, but most scholars do not see the apocalypse as a cryptogram for the remainder of history.

C. To the *futurist*, Revelation does not describe what took place in John's day, nor what is happening in ours, but refers to that which will transpire before the second coming. Generally, this school concedes that Chapters 1–3 apply to the first century, but all the rest, Chapters 4–22, to the end of time. Guthrie says: "It is better to conclude that in line with the Hebrew prophets, there are both immediate and distant points of view in this book, and that its relevance is thus historical and eschatological."

D. The viewpoint of this author is the *prophetic-apocalyptic* view. Revelation is prophetic in the sense that John spoke to his day, and to ours, and yet has a long range application to the *parousia*, or the second coming of Christ. The term, apocalyptic, is used to remind us that the events described are symbolic, and not to be interpreted in a strict literalistic fashion. This prophetic-apocalyptic interpretation includes the best of all three previous interpretations. It sees John's Revelation as rooted in the past, relevant today, and anticipatory of the great victory at the second coming. It agrees with the historicist in seeing the principles enumerated by John as relevant to the present historical scene. *Whenever* evil manifests itself, God does come to deliver. But on that *great day* Christ will completely overthrow the powers of evil. Finally, with the futurist, it sees man's ultimate hope resting only in God who will triumph through Christ as his parousia.

III. Authorship and Date

A. Authorship. Tradition is virtually unanimous in identifying the author with John, the *Beloved Apostle*, the son of Zebedee, who received the revelation while he was on the island of Patmos because of his witness to the Lord. Justin Martyr (*ca.* A.D. 100), Irenaeus (*ca.* A.D. 130), Tertullian (*ca.* A.D. 160), Clement of Alexandria (A.D. 150-213), and Origen (*cà.* A.D. 200) all ascribe it to the Apostle John. The author calls himself a "prophet" (Rev. 22:9) and our "brother," but apart from this he is silent.

Guthrie, who made a thorough study of the internal and external evidence for and against apostolic authorship, finally concludes in its favor. J. P. Love says: "Perhaps the most telling argument in favor of the writer's being John the Apostle is the harmony of the teaching of this book with the character of John as he is presented in the synoptic Gospels." There he is referred to as the "Son of Thunder" and in Revelation he presents the "thundering judgment of God." John betrayed this quality in the Gospel when he and James wanted to call down thunder on a Samaritan village (Luke 9:54). This temperament is expressed in the Apocalypse in his hostility toward the Jews (Rev. 2:9; 3:9), toward the "Beast," and the "Harlot," and in the three cycles of seven plagues which reveal the righteous judgment of God.

Some scholars object to apostolic authorship declaring that the thought, style, and the language of the Apocalypse and Gospel differ. These believe the Apocalypse is of "Hebraic Greek" composition. Guthrie points out that the Gospel has a Semitic background also, and that the thought of the two books is not radically different. The difference in style can be explained by the kind of writing and the subject matter.

When one seriously examines the content of the Apocalypse and the Gospel, the similarity becomes more obvious. Both refer to the Lord Jesus as the Word, the Lamb, and both use other terms like witness, tabernacle, keep, overcome, living water, manna, shepherd and sheep. The same Christology is essentially there — Christ is the Lamb of God who takes away our sin (John 1:29; Rev. 1:5; 5:6). Therefore, we conclude that the Apostle John wrote the Apocalypse.

B. The Date. The date most commonly accepted for the composition of the Apocalypse is about A.D. 95. Tradition (Irenaeus, Jerome, etc.) says that John was banished to Patmos to work in the mines by the ego-maniac Emperor Domitian

(A.D. 81-96). When Domitian died, the Roman Senate repealed his acts and John returned to Ephesus, either with his "revelation," or with the intention of writing it down.

Some of the reasons why a Domitian date is preferred to the earlier Neronian date are:

1. The book assumes a wide spread persecution like that of Domitian's; Nero's was localized in Rome.
2. Nero's persecution was not on religious grounds. He used the Christians merely as a scapegoat to blame for the great fire in Rome.
3. Nero did not banish Christians as Domitian did; he tortured them.
4. The degenerate conditions in the seven churches requires more time than the Neronian date permits.
5. The change in attitude toward Rome from the time of Acts as compared with Revelation fits better with a Domitian date.
6. The reference to the measuring of the temple (Rev. 11: 1 ff.) does not prove the temple was standing, but seems to be used symbolically.

As Guthrie states, when there is no internal evidence which contradicts a Domitian date of A.D. 95, it is best to stand with tradition.

IV. Destination and Purpose

A. Destination. Because he was overwhelmingly confident of Christ's immediate return and victory, John preached repentance to the "seven churches" of Asia: Ephesus, Smyrna, Pergamum, Thyatira, Sardis, Philadelphia, and Laodicea. Although these churches can be specifically identified, the fact that John only chose *seven* of the many churches in Asia, probably means that he used the number to symbolize completeness, and that his message was intended for the entire church.

B. Purpose. William Barclay makes it rather clear that the awful persecution initiated by Domitian was the worst the church had experienced to date. Christians were being called upon to join all the inhabitants of the Empire to appear before a magistrate and pledge their loyalty to Rome by offering a pinch of incense upon the altar of the Emperor Cult. Although this act was probably oriented more politically than religiously, Christians interpreted the act religiously and found it difficult to affirm "Caesar is Lord." To believers, "Jesus Christ is Lord!" He *alone* had redeemed them from bondage to sin by his vicarious sacrifice. And because of their unwillingness to compromise their faith, many Christians were banished, and many others were condemned to torturous forms of death.

It was to Christians living in times like these that the prophet John sought to minister. His message includes several themes, the most dominant one being that Christ *is* reigning as King of kings and Lord of lords in heaven and that soon he will appear to usher in the millennial kingdom and the new creation. John warns the unfaithful in the church to repent and make wrongs right, and encourages the faithful to "hold fast" to Christ until the end. Even though fidelity to Christ may result in a martyr's death, he assures the saints that the victor's crown awaits them.

It is this theme of hope which is rooted in the certain triumph of Christ that crescendos at the end of the Apocalypse when evil is completely destroyed and the eternal kingdom of God is ushered in (Rev. 20–22). It is this living hope, a hope which believers have already experienced in part through faith in Jesus Christ, that John holds before them. Although the wrong seems ever so strong, God is ruling, and he will manifest his power openly soon.

V. Eternal and Abiding Truths

As we read Revelation we cannot help but be gripped by its majesty and grandeur. A. M. Hunter has pointed out that John has a vivid sense of the majesty of God and of the centrality of Jesus Christ who triumphed through his vicarious sacrifice. The reader is compelled to affirm his faith in God's ultimate triumph over evil. There can be no doubt that John believed that history is linear and not cyclical — it is moving toward the divine destiny which God has foreordained. Although good and evil will always be engaged in apparent mortal combat in this world, some day, at God's appointed time, he will bring the curtain down and the end of this drama will mark the beginning of the eternal kingdom.

I. INTRODUCTION (1:1-3)

A. The Revelation (1:1a)

The revelation, i.e., vision and its interpretation which John sent to the churches, was not one of his own making but it was one which he received from God (cf. Gal. 1:12). The subject of the revelation and the Mediator of it was none other than Jesus Christ. It contained God's disclosure of things which "*must* soon take place." A prophet's message was primarily addressed to the people of his own day and secondarily to subsequent generations (cf. II Peter 1:10-12). John's hope for a "soon" fulfillment of his prophecy is expressed by others in the New Testament (cf. Luke 18:8; Rom. 16:20; I Cor. 7:29-31; I Peter 4:7). His message was addressed to his "servants" in the church who were undergoing trial and testings for their Lord.

B. The Messenger (1:1b-2)

Unlike apocryphal apocalyptic works which use a pseudonym, John is specifically mentioned as the prophet of God who was to convey his message to the churches. God revealed it to John through his mediating angel (cf. Dan. 7:16; 8:18 ff.). John is called a "servant," or more accurately a "slave" (*doulos*). He was bound to his Lord who ransomed him with his very life blood (1:5; cf. I Cor. 6:21). As one who was with Christ from his baptism to his ascension (Acts 1:21-22), he bore witness "to the word of God and to the testimony of Jesus Christ" (1:2). The English word "witness" in Greek is *martyr*. John and the faithful in the book of Revelation are not nominal Christians, but they are dedicated to the point of death if need be. He witnessed to the Word of God, i.e., the Old Testament prophecy and to its New Testament fulfillment in Jesus Christ.

C. The Blessing (1:3)

John pronounces a special "blessing" upon those who read his prophecy and those who hear. It was customary to read the Scriptures as a part of the worship service in the synagogue, a practice continued by the early church (Luke 4:16; Acts 13:15). Manuscripts were expensive and believers were dependent upon the reading of the Word in church for their instruction in the faith. It was a genuine privilege to hear the Word of God, a privilege which we take too lightly. The blessing which awaits the hearer is not his unless he "keeps" or "obeys" the Word.

Biblical faith is always obedient faith. It is not the hearers of the Word who receive the blessing, but those who *both hear and do* (cf. Matt. 5:21 ff.; James 1:22-25). This "blessing" or "beatitude" is the first of seven in the Apocalypse (cf. 4:13; 16:15; 19:9; 20:6; 22:7, 14).

John believed it was especially important to heed his prophecy because the "time is near," i.e., the second advent of our Lord. This ought to be the constant hope and the motivating factor in the believer's life (cf. I John 3:1-3).

II. A GENERAL LETTER TO THE SEVEN CHURCHES (1:4-20)

A. The Greeting (1:4-5a)

The seven churches which John addresses (1:4, 11) were in the Roman Province of Asia, Pergamos being the capital. Scholars are generally agreed that since the number *seven* symbolizes "wholeness" or "completeness," the seven churches represent not seven specific churches but *the church,* the entire Body of Christ.

Paul customarily opens his letters with a similar greeting (Phil. 1:2; I Cor. 1:3; etc.) as John does here. In 1:4, however, the "grace" and "peace" come from the Triune God — Father, Son, and Holy Spirit. The One "who *is* and who *was* and who *is to come*" is God the Father. This title stresses both his eternity and his vital relationship to history. The "seven spirits" which are before the throne symbolize the Holy Spirit, seven again symbolizing completeness or perfection. Jesus Christ is called the "faithful witness," the One who witnesses by his life and death to the whole truth of God (cf. John 1:14, 17; 14:6; 18:37). He is also the "first begotten" or "first born" (*prōtotokos*) from the dead (1:5). Christ was the first to be raised from the dead to a new life, and therefore, the "first fruits of them that sleep" (cf. Col. 1:18; I Cor. 15:20). The language implies the future resurrection of the saints. Finally, he is the "ruler of kings on earth" (1:5a). While his rule is not acknowledged by the world, it is by the body of believers, and it will be by the world at his second advent (17:14). "Thus his sacrifice, his resurrection, and his eternal reign are combined at the very outset" (Love).

B. The Doxology (1:5b-6)

Now John lifts his voice in grateful praise to Jesus Christ our Redeemer who "freed us from our sins." For other "doxologies" in Revelation see 5:12-13; 7:10. It is interesting to note that the tense of the verb "love" (*agapōnti*) suggests our Lord's love continuously manifested, at Calvary and subsequently. The verb "freed" (*lusanti*), however, is in the aorist tense and emphasizes the "once for all time" nature of the act of redemption. Our Lord loosed us from the penalty of our sin (cf. Col. 1:14; I Peter 1:19). The price of our redemption was his very life blood (cf. Heb. 7:27; 10:11 ff.). By the act of redemption we *are made* a "kingdom *of* priests" to God. We are reminded here of the old covenant made between Israel and God (Exod. 19:5-6). Christ has ushered in the new covenant by his sacrifice, thereby delivering us from a foe greater than any physical one: he delivered us from bondage to sin and Satan (Heb. 8:1-13; 2:14-15). Believers are presently constituted a royal priesthood with both the privilege of access to the throne of grace, and the responsibility of intercession for others (Heb. 10:19-22; 4:16; I Peter 3:5, 9, 18).

As priests of God we are to be God-centered in our living, i.e., our chief purpose in life is to serve and glorify God our Father (1:6). But here John is not referring to our present priesthood, but "to the reign of the saints and their priesthood in the messianic kingdom when it is established" (cf. 3:10; 20:6) (Beckwith).

C. The Second Advent (1:7-8)

The "blessed hope" of Christ's return is affirmed in words similar to Matt. 24:30, derived from Daniel 7:13 and Zechariah 12:10-12. Christ will come with judgment against "all nations," both Jew and Gentile, who have crucified him (John 1:10 f.; I John 5:19). This prophecy will be fulfilled at Christ's final victory over the forces of evil as pictured in 19:11-21. Man has a choice of responding to God as he confronts him in Christ in one of two ways, he may *either* accept him as Savior and Lord, *or* he will face Christ as judge (Luke 20:18; Rom. 2:16; Phil. 2:9-11). To this announcement of the Lord's return the prophet responds with enthusiastic approval — "Even so, Amen!"

Verse 8 makes it clear that it is the Lord God Almighty who has announced Christ's soon return. *Alpha and Omega* are the first and last letters of the Greek alphabet and are probably a translation of the Hebrew idiom, *Aleph and Tau,* the first and last letters of the Hebrew alphabet. This expression aptly suggests the entirety of a thing. Here John couples it with the three tenses of the copula "is, was, is to come." The Lord God of history at the very outset assures the saints of final triumph. Cf. 22:13 where the same saying is attributed to Christ.

D. The Initial Vision (1:9-20)

1. John on Patmos (1:9-11). Note the modesty of this "son of thunder." He does not lay claim to his title of *Apostle,* but merely identifies himself with his brethren in their suffering. Truly he could empathize with them for he, too, was "sharing in the sufferings of Christ." Paul, John, and others in the early

church felt that suffering for Christ was part of their mission and a condition for entrance into the kingdom (cf. Acts 14:22; Phil. 1:29; II Tim. 2:12). John brings together here both the "tribulation" (*thlipsei*) and the "kingdom" (*basileia*), two of the dominant ideas of this book. The tribulation is a present experience as is also the kingdom, but it is also a future hope. Only those with "patient endurance" will enter into its fullness (cf. Mark 13:13). As Christians we must learn to be patient in tribulation as God exercises his rule in our hearts, for even in the midst of the world we can know victory over the evil one (cf. John 16:33; I John 5:4-5).

It was on Patmos, that rugged prison island off the coast of Ephesus, that John *was* banished for preaching "the word of God and the testimony of Jesus" (1:9; cf. 6:9; 12:17; 19:10; 20:4). Ezekiel has a similar experience; he had been exiled to the river Chebar and it was as he "sat where they [his brethren] sat" that God gave him his revelation (3:15). Some think that John's use of the past tense, *was*, indicates that he only received his revelation on Patmos and that it was not until later, after he was off the island, that he wrote the Apocalypse.

John was "in the Spirit" on the "Lord's day" when he heard the crystal clear voice speak to him commanding him to write down his vision in a book and send it to the seven churches. "In the Spirit" (*en pneumati*) means that he was caught up by the Spirit in an ecstatic experience (cf. 4:2; 17:3; 21:10). This experience occurred on the "Lord's day," the day when believers celebrated Christ's victory over the grave — his glorious resurrection (cf. I Cor. 16:2; Acts 20:7). John is the first to use this expression which became an earlier designation for the first day of the week. Adolph Deissmann has suggested that Christians deliberately used this designation to make it clear to the people of Asia, who celebrated the first day of the week as the "Emperor's Day," that they worshipped *Jesus Christ as Lord* and not Caesar.

Not only was John to write his initial vision (1:12-20), but all subsequent revelations (1:19), and send them as a circular letter to the seven churches of Asia (Ephesus, Smyrna, Pergamum, Thyatire, Sardis, Philadelphia, and Laodicea). Tradition associates the Apostle John with the city of Ephesus and it is not unlikely that his leadership extended to these churches which William Ramsay says formed a semi-circular route around the province of Asia. Ramsay also suggests that these cities were centers of seven postal districts which might account for their choice. Ephesus was the chief city in the province of Asia and this would account for its place at the head of the list.

2. The Son of Man Amid the Churches (1:12-20). John now records his vision of the Christ — the Son of Man — who stands amidst the churches, the lampstands (1:12-13). The Apostle wants to assure the churches that the victorious Christ is the source of their light and strength. I am following J. P. Love who divides this vision into three parts.

a. His Character (1:12-15). When John heard the "voice" (cf. 1:17 ff.) speaking to him, he turned and saw "seven golden lampstands." In the Old Testament the seven pronged lamp was kept in the holy place of the tabernacle and later in the temple (Exod. 25:31; Zech. 4:2). When the temple was destroyed by Titus it was taken to a heathen temple in Rome. The lampstand symbolized Israel of old, God's chosen people who, supplied by divine oil, were to be a light to the nations (Isa. 49:6). Now the lampstands symbolize the church of Jesus Christ, the new Israel of God. Christ is the light of the world (John 8:12), even as God the Father is light (I John 1:5). As children of God, redeemed by Christ, we, too, are "children of the light," and we are to let his light shine through us in order that he might be glorified (John 12:36; Eph. 5:8; I Thess. 5:5; Matt. 5:14-16).

In the midst of these lampstands, churches, stood one like a Son of Man (1:13). This was our Lord's self-designation (Mark 10:45). He fused the concept of the Suffering Servant of Isaiah with that of the Son of Man found in Daniel. In his first advent he suffered, but now he occupies a place of honor and authority at God's right hand (Acts 3:13 ff.; 4:27 ff.; 7:55-56). The Son of Man is seen possessing the attributes of God which are found in Daniel 7:13; 10:5-6. The "long robe" suggests his authority and dignity. It may be a judicial robe symbolizing that Christ is the One who will judge men and nations, as well as the church. The "golden girdle" around the breast suggests his priestly work. The "white" head and hair symbolizes the Son of Man's purity, wisdom and divinity (1:14). His "eyes" like a flaming fire symbolize his penetrating vision and discerning judgment. His feet of "burnished bronze" suggest his strength to overcome all opposition. His voice which was "like the sound of many waters" symbolizes his irresistible power and fullness with which the Son of Man now speaks (cf. Ezek. 43:2).

b. His Ministry (1:16-17a). Beasley-Murray rightly reminds

us that this picture of the Son of Man in 1:16 was never meant to be painted. But it was meant to, and it does, convey the truth of Christ's sustaining power within the church and of his judgment against her enemies. The "seven stars" which John says are the "angels" of the seven churches are "held in his right hand." In his Gospel John says that the believer is secure in Christ's hands; therefore, this is true of the church also (John 10:28-30).

The "two edged sword" which issues from his mouth speaks of Christ's judicial power and might both inside and outside the church (cf. Isa. 49:2-7; Heb. 4:12; II Thess. 2:8). This Word of Christ is able to lay us bare before him — it strips away all sham and hypocrisy. But it is only as we submit to his Word that we are made whole.

But the Son of Man is gracious, too. John says that "his face was like the sun shining in full strength." He may be alluding to Judges 5:4, but most interpreters see a reference to the Mount of Transfiguration where our Lord's face is said to have "shone like the sun" (Matt. 17:2). John was there — he experienced this foretaste of glory. It would not be amiss to see here also an allusion to the glorious truth which Paul laid hold of when he said that "the God who said, 'Let light shine out of darkness,' . . . has shone in our hearts to give the light of the knowledge of the glory of God in the face of Jesus Christ" (II Cor. 4:6). Thus judgment and redemption are both part of his ministry.

c. His Resources (1:17b-18). At the presence of such an awesome vision John prostrates himself, even as other prophets who were privileged to have visions (1:17a; cf. Ezek. 1:28; Dan. 8:17; 10:9; Isa. 6:5 ff.). But the Christ speaks reassuringly to John. Christ, "the first and the last, and the living one" now speaks, ascribing to himself the rightful qualities of the Deity. We saw how "first" and "last" were applied to God (Isa. 44:6; Rev. 1:8), but now our Lord uses an expression of himself — "the living one" — which Jewish literature often ascribed to God the Father. As John said elsewhere (John 5:26), "as the Father has life in himself, so he has granted the Son also to have life in himself." By virtue of his victory in his cross-resurrection-ascension he has conquered death and hell (1:18; cf. Rom. 1:4), and in him we are victorious, too (17:14). Not only has our Lord conquered death, but he has also given us the keys to the kingdom that we, too, might lead men out of death into life (cf. Matt. 16:19; John 20:23; Acts 26:18; Eph. 2:2).

3. The Structure of the Book (1:19). The *Apocalypse* is divided into three sections by John: (1) literally "what you have seen," i.e., the introduction and the vision of the Son of Man (chap. 1); (2) "what is," i.e., the condition of the seven churches revealed in the letters (chaps. 2–3); and finally (3) "what is to take place hereafter" (chaps. 4–22). Some divide the book as follows: chaps. 1–3 ("what you have seen"); chaps. 4–5 ("what is"); chaps. 6–22; ("what is to take place hereafter").

Although scholars do agree that the symbolism of the lampstands represents the seven churches, they are not unanimous in their interpretation of the "seven stars." All John tells us is that the seven stars are the "angels of the seven churches." Zahn and Weiss identify the "angel" with the "teacher" or "overseer" of the particular churches. But "angels" (*angelis*) almost never symbolizes men in Revelation and in other apocalyptic literature. Other scholars take the angel to refer to the "guardian angel" of the churches. Guardian angels are ascribed to persons and nations (cf. Matt. 18:10; Acts 12:15; Dan. 10:13, 20), so one might conceive of a church having a guardian angel in heaven as Origen, Porter, and Moffatt have suggested. But Christ addresses the churches, *not* an intermediary. Finally, the view of Swete, Beasley-Murray, and Beckwith is that the "angel of a church is equivalent to the church itself, or its personified life." The "lampstands" represent the church visible while the "angels" symbolize its "invisible spiritual life." This seems like the most probable interpretation.

III. THE LETTERS TO THE SEVEN CHURCHES (2:1–3:22)

When Christ addresses these seven churches he addresses them as a *true* pastor or shepherd. He does not close his eyes to what is good or evil, but he seeks to commend them wherein they have been faithful and condemn them wherein they have and are failing in their mission. As a genuine pastor our Lord calls them to repentance, ever holding out to them the forgiving love of God, but not failing to warn them of the impending doom if they fail to do so.

One unique feature of each letter is the way in which the prophet begins with some appropriate part of the vision of the Son of Man which meets the needs of the particular church. Only in the case of the church at Laodicea does he seem to go back to the introduction of the Revelation. Appropriately the letters close with a promise of eternal blessings at the parousia.

As the reader meditates upon the life-situation of these churches, doubtlessly he will find many parallels between the church of the first century and that in our own time. We should remember that the Christ is still in the midst of the churches today to strengthen, commend, judge, call to repentance, restore and use her to bring glory to God.

In presenting the material content of the letters we shall divide it into five sections: (1) the city, (2) the commendation, (3) the condemnation, (4) the call to repentance, (5) the blessing.

A. The Letter to the Church at Ephesus (2:1-7)

1. The City of Ephesus. Ephesus was the foremost city of Asia even though Pergamum was the capital. Since it was the gateway to Asia and Rome, it was an important commercial, political and religious center. It has been called the "Market of Asia," and the "Vanity Fair" of the ancient world. A temple to Artemus (Diana), one of the seven wonders of the ancient world, was located there (Acts 19:35). Ephesus was also one of the chief seats of the Emperor Cult. It was in this city that Apollos and Aquilla and Priscilla had earlier labored, so that when Paul appeared later he found a group of John the Baptist's disciples and he led them into a full knowledge of Jesus as the Christ (Acts 19:1 ff.). Here Paul stayed for three years, faithfully preaching the gospel (Acts 20:11-41).

Tradition has it that John had a fruitful ministry at Ephesus, and brought Mary the mother of Jesus there to live. Both are believed to have died at Ephesus.

John probably addressed them first because of the strategic importance of the Ephesian church and, as Kiddle suggests, because of the important warning given.

Christ encourages the Ephesians, and the other churches, by reminding them that it is he who holds them (2:1; cf. I Peter 1:5). The force of the word "holds" (*kratōn*) suggests "complete control." It is none other than the Christ who walks continually amidst the churches, keeping constant vigil over his own. He is there to both encourage, strengthen and judge.

2. The Commendation (2:2-3, 6). The message of Christ is related to the church's problem and need. It seems as though some itinerant preachers known as Nicolaitans had gained entrance into the churches and probably had led some into idolatry and immorality. Some scholars have suggested that these teachers were followers of Nicolas of Antioch, one of the seven mentioned in Acts 6:5, but there is no real evidence to support this assumption. Whatever the nature of the heresy, the Ephesians had successfully (?) resisted it and remained true to the faith.

Christ commends them for their "works" (*erga*), "hard toil" (*kopon*), and their "patient endurance" (*hupomonēn*). "Works" includes more than deeds, it refers to their "life and conduct in general, including both outward and spiritual activities." Their hard toil was demonstrated in their resistance to the apostate teachers (2:6). Likewise, their patient endurance is seen in their willingness to bear all manner of trials for Christ's sake. They have resisted the "false apostles" of whom Paul had forewarned the church (Acts 20:29), by testing them (2:2-3; I John 4:1). In their fight against licentiousness and false doctrine they had not grown weary (2:3).

3. The Condemnation (2:4). But as often happens when individuals and churches become involved in defending the faith, the Ephesian church "abandoned the love" they "had at first," or "their first love" (2:4). The "love" (*agapēn*) here is usually understood as not love for Christ *per se,* but love for the brethren, which is the genuine manifestation of *agape.* This is a constant theme of Christ and John — love for God and Christ must practically demonstrate itself in love of the brethren, otherwise the claim to faith is merely a pretense, a sham (cf. I John 3:11 ff., 17-18; John 13:34-35; Matt. 5:43-48). While it is true that we must stand fast in the faith, we must

ever be on guard against loosing the fruit of the Spirit, *agape*, while holding fast to the "creed."

4. The Call to Repentance (2:5). "Remember," "repent," "do" are present imperatives which call for decisive continued response. Swete notes that these verbs denote three stages of conversion and spiritual renewal. The Ephesians are to constantly recall the fellowship of love they enjoyed by virtue of being in fellowship with the living God in Christ, then to repent, i.e., turn from the sins which have led them astray, and finally they are to continue to do the "good works" characteristic of those in fellowship with God (2:4a).

Christ says "I will come" with judgment and remove your lampstand from among the churches unless they repent! When a church loses its love for the brethren, then it ceases to be a church. John said elsewhere substantially the same thing under the allegory of the Vine and the Branches (John 15:1 ff.; cf. Matt. 7:21-23).

5. The Blessing (2:7). Our lord speaks to the prophet through the Holy Spirit (1:7a) calling each individual to "hear" and respond to the call to repentance. He frequently appealed to his hearers to be careful how they heard (cf. Matt. 13:9, 43, etc.), and even now he makes the same appeal in each letter. To those who hear, i.e., respond in repentance and obedience, Christ promises the privilege of eating of the "tree of life" which is in the "paradise of God." It is obvious that our Lord is here referring to the tree of life in the Garden of Eden from which our disobedient, rebellious "parents" were expelled (cf. Gen. 3:22-24; Rev. 22:2; Ezek. 47:12). All who overcome, not only the martyrs of the first century, will share in the joys of the fullness of the eternal kingdom.

B. The Letter to the Church at Smyrna (2:8-11)

1. The City of Smyrna. Smyrna and Philadelphia are the only two churches for which our Lord has nothing but commendation. It was a real metropolis with one of the largest populations in Asia and it has been called by Lucian "the fairest of the cities of Ionia." Located to the north of Ephesus, with a safe land-locked harbor, the city was a throbbing center of trade. The city was also known as a center of culture. It claimed to be the birth place of Homer. Religiously it was a center of Emperor worship, having been the first city in the world to erect a temple to the goddess Roma and later (A.D. 26) one to the Emperor Tiberius. Among its populace were a

large number of Jews who were hostile to the Christian community (2:9).

It was here that Polycarp, bishop of Smyrna, served Christ so long and faithfully. When he was given the choice to either renounce Christ or die, Polycarp replied, "Eighty and six years have I served Him and He has done me no wrong. How can I blaspheme my King who saved me?" And so he was martyred, February 23, A.D. 155.

Therefore the Smyrnan church, like many churches in atheistic totalitarian lands since then, has had to battle with a hostile environment which sought to crush it.

Humanly speaking one would not expect a strong church at Smyrna, for not only was the Jewish persecution bitter, but the people were materially poor. But as is often the case, privation and persecution produced a strong faith. Compare Christ's words to this "poor" church with his message to the "rich" church at Laodicea (3:14-22).

The introduction (2:8) is tailor-made to the people's needs. As they perhaps are seeing their members imprisoned and facing martyrdom, our Lord reminds them that he is the one "who died and came to life," he is the first and the last. We are reminded of his words to his disciples when he was on earth: ". . . do not fear those who kill the body, . . . But fear him who, after he has killed, has power to cast into hell" (Luke 12:4-5). The Smyrnans can trust, without wavering, the Lord of history who will vindicate them on *that day.*

2. The Commendation (2:9-10b). The Lord commends this church for her patient endurance in the midst of bitter persecution (2:9). But Christ "knows" their plight; he knows the "tribulation" and "poverty" and "slander" (blasphemy) they endure at the hands of those who call themselves Jews. This "tribulation" is not merely the persecution many associate with the end-time, but it was that which they were experiencing then. Wherever the church dares to stand for Christ it will suffer tribulation, but in and through the power of Christ it will be victorious (cf. John 16:33; I John 5:4-5). The poverty of the Smyrnan church was due to the fact that many of the early Christians came from the lower classes of society and from the slaves. Some interpreters feel that their poverty was due to discrimination and boycotts on the part of the non-Christians. But the believers were rich in faith and possessed an inheritance which money could not buy. (Cf. Rev. 3:15-22 where the Laodicean church had material wealth but was spiritually poor.)

In the first century the persecution most often originated from the Jews who refused to accept Jesus as the Messiah and therefore persecuted those who preached Christ. Paul had said that "he is not a real Jew who is one outwardly, nor is true circumcision something external and physical" (Rom. 2:28). John recorded in his gospel the hostility of the Jews toward Christ, and now our Lord says that those who parade as Jews are none other than members of the synagogue of Satan (2:9; 3:9; cf. John 8:39 ff.). But these Jews and the Romans are not to receive all the credit for the persecution of the church, for they are being used by the Devil (*diabolos*) to persecute the saints. The origin of this testing is from God. The length of the persecution is fixed — "ten days" (2:10b). Ten is a round number which denotes "fullness" or "completeness." This period of persecution will not be long, but it will be long enough to prove their dedication to Christ. In the *last days* a world wide persecution will break out, but here a local persecution seems to be in view (cf. 3:10).

3. The Blessing (2:10c-11). Jesus holds before the suffering saints the promise of certain victory. Even though they may die, they can face death with confidence, knowing that "the crown of life" awaits them (2:10c; cf. James 1:12). The obvious meaning is that the crown symbolizes "everlasting life," the ultimate reward of victory. The Hebrews often used the word crown metaphorically to denote honor and dignity (Ps. 8:5; 103:4; Job 31:36), and in the New Testament it is used as here in Revelation to symbolize the eschatological reward, victory over evil (cf. I Cor. 9:25; II Tim. 4:8; James 1:12).

Not only will the saints receive the "crown of life," but they will not be affected by the "second death" (2:11). The first death is the natural death to which all men are subjected, whereas the second death is eternal separation from God which will befall all those who reject the Christ. This sentence of "second death" will be meted out at the Great White Throne Judgment (20:6, 14; 21:8). Believers who have been born again and who have been obedient to the Lord, however, need never fear death, neither the first, nor the second (John 3:3; 11:25-26).

C. The Letter to the Church at Pergamum (2:13-17)

1. The City of Pergamum. The city of Pergamum (or Pergamus) was the capital of the province of Asia and, although it was not as important as Ephesus commercially, as a political, religious and cultural city it was, perhaps, second to

none. Its library numbered 200,000 rolls, second in size only to that at Alexandria. Here the seat of Emperor worship was located, the first temple to the Emperor Augustus being built in A.D. 29. At Pergamum were also shrines to Zeus, Athene, Dionysus, and Asklepios, the god of health and healing. Connected with the shrine of Asklepios was the medical college for priests. It was to this shrine that sufferers from all over the Mediterranean gathered. R. H. Charles called Pergamum "the Lourdes of the ancient world."

Because Pergamum was the center for the Emperor cult in Asia, Christ refers to it as "Satan's seat." Many Christians were to be added to the list of martyrs because they, like Antipas, refused to worship the Emperor by saying "Caesar is Lord" (2:13).

Even though the governor at Pergamum had the "right to the sword," John is reminded that it is Christ who has the "two edged sword" which he will wield on that day (2:12).

2. The Commendation (2:13). Christ praises the believers here because despite the presence of the Emperor cult and other pagan shrines, despite the fact that some have bowed the knee to the teachings of the "Balaamites" and the "Nicolaitans," most of them "are holding fast" (*krateis*) to the name of Christ. The aorist tense is used here and, therefore, alludes to a specific testing through which the Pergamene church has passed (2:13). One of their number, Antipas, chose martyrdom rather than life without Christ (2:13).

3. The Condemnation (2:14-15). But despite the heroism of most, there are some at Pergamum who have been led astray. The false teachers are not outsiders who are seeking to gain entrance as at Ephesus (2:2), but they are right there in the church. The teaching of Balaam in Numbers (25:1 ff.; 31:16) led Balak to put a "stumbling-block" (*skandalon*) before Israel. Through the worship of the fertility god, Baal, Israel had not only been led into idolatry but also to commit fornication. So, says Christ, "you also have some who hold the teaching of the Nicolaitans" (2:15). Most interpreters understand here that there is only one group of false teachers, the Nicolaitans, who are comparable to Balaam of old. Idolatry of any sort results in immorality of some kind. Man cannot turn from God in Christ without expecting to pay for it in one way or another (cf. Gal. 6:7).

4. The Call to Repentance (2:16). Christ calls them to repent of their toleration of the false Nicolaitan teachers and

cast them out. If they do not, Christ threatens to come with judgment against these false teachers *and* the church for their leniency toward them. Christ will judge them with the sword of his mouth (1:15).

5. The Blessing (2:17). Quite appropriately our Lord promises the Christians at Pergamum, who are being tempted to leave him to participate in the banqueting of the Nicolaitans, that those who "overcome" (*nikōnti*) will be given some of the "hidden manna." A belief current among the Jews was that when the Messiah came manna would again descend from heaven (II Baruch 29:8). Doubtlessly manna is used here as a symbol of the promised blessings which await the believer at the coming of Christ and the fullness of the kingdom. Although the blessing is "hidden" now, it will be manifest at his coming.

"A white stone" with "a new name" will be given the "overcomers," i.e., the believers, who resist steadfastly to the end (2:17). In the ancient world white stones with the name of a deity were used as amulets to ward off demons, they were given to one acquitted at a trial, and they were given to victors at the games as a "ticket" to admit him to public festivals, etc. Here Christ is probably alluding to a pagan custom familiar to the church, and he is saying that if they are victors in the "Christian race" they will be given "a white stone," a symbol of purity and victory, and upon it will be a "new name." This "new name" may be that of Christ, or of God, which would suggest that their power is given to the believer, or the new name may be the new name given to the believer upon his entrance into a new life in Christ. Beasley-Murray seems to suggest both. The white stone with the new name gains us entrance into the eternal kingdom, and by God's name, power, we are enabled to overcome evil (Swete, Moffatt, etc.). Only the believer knows this name of the One True God and experiences the riches of his grace (cf. I Cor. 2:9-10).

D. The Letter to the Church at Thyatira (2:18-29)

1. The City of Thyatira. Thyatira, the smallest of the seven cities, was known primarily for its dyeing and woolen industries. Beckwith suggests that Lydia, "a seller of purple" (Acts 16:14 f.) may have been an agent of a Thyatirian business house. The church in that city was probably established by Paul during his extended stay in Asia (Acts 19:10). The church, like many others, was probably predominantly composed of Gentiles, since the Jews are not mentioned.

The city was noted for its "trade guilds" and it was around these that the trouble centered. If one wished to enter a trade or advance in it, he had to belong to the "trade guild" peculiar to his skill. Unfortunately, these guilds usually had a patron deity, and connected with the guild's activities were communial meals in the temples which began and ended with sacrifices to the deity. Drinking and sexual immorality were usually associated with the festivities at the temple. Because the Christians felt compelled not to join the guilds they found themselves ostracized and boycotted. Because earning a livelihood was so difficult outside the trade guilds many Christians were tempted to compromise their faith; after all, had Paul not said that an "idol is nothing"? The temptation was heightened by the presence of a false prophetess whom they called "Jezebel," and who seemed to be counseling Christians to acquiesce to the temptation (2:20). The crucial nature of the problem at Thyatira accounts for the length of this letter, the longest of the seven.

The Christ who introduces his message to the heresy-ridden church is seen by John and described as "the Son of God, who has eyes like a flame of fire . . . feet . . . like burnished bronze" (2:18). Psalm 2:7-9 is the background for Christ's words. He is the Messiah to whom judgment has been committed. His piercing eyes see through the falseness of "Jezebel's" teaching, and he promises to come with judgment to treat his enemies under his feet (2:18, 22-23).

2. The Commendation (2:19). The commendable thing about this church is its "works." Charles suggests that the works are defined as love, faith, service, and patient endurance (2:19). Beckwith, however, sees but two works: love and faithfulness. The love manifesting itself in service and the faith in steadfast endurance. The fruitfulness of these Christians was on the increase, and unlike the church at Laodicea which remained static, the Thyatireans were doing more for Christ now than they had heretofore (2:19).

3. The Condemnation (2:20-24). "Jezebel." Although some manuscripts read "thy wife Jezebel," thereby suggesting that Jezebel symbolizes the wife of the "angel," i.e., the messenger or pastor of the church, most scholars prefer the Revised Standard Version rendering, "the woman Jezebel." As the Nicolaitans were compared with Balaam, so the apostate teacher at Thyatira is compared with the nefarious Old Testament character Jezebel (cf. I Kings 16:29 ff.; II Kings 9:22). Jezebel not only was responsible for the downfall of Ahab, but eventually for all of Israel.

The reason Christ was so severe with Jezebel was because prophets occupied such a prominent place in the early church, even as they did in Israel (cf. Acts 11:27; 13:1; I Cor. 12:28; 14:1 ff.; Eph. 4:11). Since this woman claimed the prophet's character and authority, her teaching was all the more undermining to genuine Christian commitment. She, like the Nicolaitans, was leading believers into idolatry and immorality (fornication), despite the fact that Christ confronted her, warned her, and gave her time to repent. Just how Christ confronted her — by messenger, letter, etc. — is not stated (2:21).

Because she persistently refuses to repent, Christ, using language understandable by one practicing such vice, says that he will throw her and her followers upon a "sickbed" and "into great tribulation." These two expressions are parallel, thereby saying that both she and her disciples will "suffer affliction." With Charles, we should see two groups of Jezebel's disciples. "Those who commit adultery with her" are probably those Christians who compromise their faith, whereas "her children" are probably those who have sold out to her diabolical doctrine and practices, body and soul (2:23a).

The teachings of Jezebel are referred to as "the deep things of Satan" (2:24). This reference is frequently interpreted as "an ironical attack upon an incipient Gnosticism." Gnostics were those who believed that God had vouchsafed to them some "special knowledge" which *ipso facto* made them children of God. Often they were libertines, since they were dualistic, insisting that while the "spiritual" was good and eternal, the flesh was evil and temporal. One such group was the *Ophites* of Syria, whose symbol, the serpent, was believed to be a supreme emanation of God.

4. The Call to Repentance (2:22-25). Although no explicit call to repentance is given, it is implicit. The church is "tolerating" Jezebel, i.e., they are permitting her to occupy a place in their midst. If they are to inherit the blessing of the messianic kingdom they must act now. Christ reminds them that he sees into the very heart and mind of men; he knows not only their thoughts, but also the intents of their hearts (2:23). The background of 2:23 is Jeremiah 17:10:

> I, the Lord, search the mind and try the heart,
> to give to every man according to his ways,
> according to the fruit of his doings.

Since Christ is God, his reward on *that day* will be just; his reward will not be based upon outward appearances. Each will be rewarded according to his works (cf. Matt. 25:31-46; II Cor. 5:10; Rev. 20:12).

To those who had been faithful Christ says, "I do not lay upon you any other burden; only hold fast what you have, until I come" (2:24-25). At the Jerusalem Council (Acts 15:28-29) the church had agreed that although the ceremonial law of Israel was not binding, both Gentile and Jewish Christians should "abstain from what has been sacrificed to idols . . . and from fornication." The added incentive to "hold fast" until the end is the reward awaiting the faithful.

5. The Blessing (2:26-28). To those who conquer, i.e., overcome the temptations of Jezebel and keep performing good works until Christ returns, will be given power by Christ and they will participate with him in the overthrow of the forces of evil (2:26-27; cf. 19:11 f.). Our Lord is referring to Psalm 2:8-9. The strong language and symbolism is used because of the severity of the corruption within the church.

But more precious to the suffering saints at Thyatira is the promise that they shall be given "the morning star." In 22:16 our Lord calls himself the "bright and morning star." Our Lord is probably suggesting here that the victor will share also in the glory of the kingdom. We shall share in, and reflect, his glory (2:28).

Note that the admonition to hear follows the blessing in the last four letters (2:29).

E. The Letter to the Church at Sardis (3:1-6)

1. The City of Sardis. Sardis was a morally degenerate city. Her greatest king was Croesus (6th Cent. B.C.). His wealth is commemorated in the proverb, "As rich as Croesus." Solon, the Athenian sage and lawgiver, visited Sardis in the days of Croesus and when he saw the degeneracy of the people, he predicted the city's downfall. It fell to the armies of Cyrus of Persia who penetrated Sardis' "impenetrable" fortifications. The city flourished for a while under the Greeks, but it degenerated once again.

After an earthquake in A.D. 17 which leveled the city to the ground, the Emperor Tiberius remitted the city's taxes for five years and gave them funds to rebuild. Under the Romans it became an important industrial center, famous for dyeing and woolen industries. It was also made the assize town, the seat of the Roman provincial courts.

But just as many individuals are never able to break the grip of some besetting sin, so Sardis never freed herself from her moral profligacy. Swete says: "The atmosphere of an old pagan city, heavy with the immoral traditions of eight centuries, was unfavorable to the growth of her spiritual life."

Christ's introduction to the Sardinean church is twofold; he reminds them that he "has the seven spirits of God" (omniscience, cf. 5:6), and he has "the seven stars" (he is head of the church). Christ is fully aware of the spiritual slumber of the church at Sardis. Although they may have a "form" of godliness, there is no real power or substance there (3:1; cf. II Tim. 3:5). Not only does he have the seven spirits, but he also has "the seven stars" (cf. 1:4, 16). Christ wishes to remind the Sardinean Christians that he is the Head of the Church. It is he who walks among them, and unless they awake to their responsibility, he will come with judgment upon them.

2. The Commendation (3:4). This is a pathetic church; there is not much good that can be said about it. Fortunately for Sardis there were a few "who had not soiled their garments." The soiled garments do not symbolize unchastity, *per se*, instead, they refer to "contamination in general" which results from yielding to the many temptations in their society. (Jude 23). Note the appropriateness of Christ's commendation. In this thriving garment center there were some who had kept themselves pure. These shall be clothed in white, the sign of victory and purity, and they will walk in intimate fellowship with Christ in his eternal kingdom (cf. Matt. 22:1-14).

3. The Condemnation (3:1b-2). Like many a Pharisee in Christ's day and in ours, the Christians at Sardis were resting on the laurels of believers who had long since gone. Christ knew their true condition. "Dead (*nekros*) is not to be interpreted as complete spiritual death, but as "on the point of death" as 3:2 suggests.

Christ calls them to "awake and strengthen what remains" (cf. Eph. 5:14). The church as a whole has been weighed in the balances and found wanting. Their works, i.e., "their characteristic spiritual life as a whole," have not been found to be perfected or fulfilled (*peplērōmena*) (cf. Dan. 5:27).

4. The Call to Repentance (3:3). Beasley-Murray calls special attention to the tenses in 3:3: "Keep in mind (present) how you received and still hold on to the gift of God (perfect) and how you gave a hearing (aorist) to the gospel; continue to hold fast (present) and bring yourself to repentance (aorist)."

If the church refuses to awake from her stupor, Christ promises to come with judgment at a time when they least expect it — as a thief comes in the night (3:3; cf. 16:15; Matt. 24:43; I Thess. 5:2; II Peter 3:10). Just as there was a decisive hour (ōran) for Christ to go to Calvary to redeem men, so he will come at the appointed time to reward the faithful and punish the unfaithful and unbelieving (cf. John 12:23 ff.; 5:28 f.; Heb. 9:28).

5. The Blessing (3:5-6). The blessing awaiting the faithful who conquer evil in Christ's name is threefold: (1) he will be clad in a white garment; (2) his name will be written in the book of life; (3) and his name will be confessed before the Father and the angels. "White garments" here symbolize ethical purity and victory, as mentioned earlier. But it also refers to the resurrection body with which the believer will be clad (cf. 4:4; II Cor. 5:4).

"The book of life" is first referred to by Moses in Exodus (32:32) where he asks God to spare the rebellious Hebrews, and not to blot their name out of the book of life, but his. Hebrew-Christian literature, apocryphal and canonical, is replete with the idea that God keeps a book in which his people's names are recorded (cf. Ps. 69:28; Dan. 12:1; I Enoch 47:3; 104:1; Matt. 10:20; Phil. 4:3; Rev. 13:8; 20:12-15). Faithful believers at Sardis can rest secure in the knowledge that their names are inscribed in the book of God's eternal kingdom. And finally, they can be confident that as they have confessed Christ before men, so he will confess them before the Father on that great day (cf. Matt. 10:32).

F. The Letter to the Church at Philadelphia (3:7-13)

1. The City of Philadelphia. The church at Philadelphia was founded by colonists under Attalus II who ruled Pergamum from 159-138 B.C. The name Philadelphia means "one who loves his brother," or "brotherly love." Attalus named it after his brother Philadelphos. The city was located on the edge of a great fertile plain, and it was famous for its grapes.

Barclay tells us that Philadelphia was plagued with earthquake tremors. The great earthquake of A.D. 17 which leveled Sardis was followed by ten years of tremors which kept the citizens always on the alert to "move out" (cf. 3:12). The city was also renamed several times, but the name of Philadelphia was finally resumed. This may account for Christ's promise that believers would have written upon them a "new name."

In the city there were a number of Jews who persecuted the Christians, claiming that they were the *true* Jews. Christ in addressing the church, therefore, declares that the Jews who rejected him, the One who has "the key of David" (3:7), are really of the "synagogue of Satan" (3:9; cf. 2:9).

The titles Christ used to introduce himself are those ascribed to God and to the Messiah. The title "the Holy One" is used elsewhere of God (4:8; 6:10), but it is used here as a designation of our Lord as the Messiah. Frequently when Jesus walked on earth he was hailed as "the Holy One" or "the Holy One of God" (cf. Mark 1:24; Luke 4:34; John 6:69; Acts 4:27, 30). He also refers to himself as "the true one," i.e., the true Messiah, the genuine one (cf. John 1:9; I John 5:20). Those of "the synagogue of Satan" do not acknowledge him as the Messiah, but they will be compelled to do so some day soon (3:9).

Christ also says that he possesses "the key of David," i.e., the key of David's house or the Messiah's kingdom. "Christ is the Davidic Messiah, who will receive his own and give them a share in his kingdom" (cf. 2:26; 3:31; 5:5; 19:11-16; 20:4; 22:16). Only "the Lion of the tribe of Judah" who was slain, can either open or shut the door of the kingdom to anyone (cf. Isa. 22:22; Rev. 5:5 ff.). No self-styled child of Abraham can enter, but only he who is circumcized of heart and confesses Christ as Lord (cf. Rom. 2:28-29; 10:9-10).

2. The Commendation (3:8-9). Even though the church at Philadelphia was small in number, and had "little strength," yet Christ commended it because it had "kept" and "not denied" his name. The "little strength" or "power" (*dunatai*) referred to does not refer to spiritual strength, but to numbers, material wealth and influence. On a given occasion they were tried, sorely tempted to deny Christ, but they "held fast" to Christ and did not deny his name, as the aorist tense suggests (3:8).

The sentence, "Behold, I have set before you an open door, which no one is able to shut," is regarded by most interpreters as a parenthesis. The "open door" can be interpreted in one of two ways: (1) as an opportunity to preach the gospel (cf. I Cor. 16:6; II Cor. 2:12; Col. 4:3); or (2) as admission into a place or state (cf. 3:20; 4:1; Acts 14:27; John 10:7, 9). It is the latter sense which is appropriate here. Christ assures the faithful that the door into his kingdom is open to them and no one can rob them of the right of entrance.

But what of those Jews of the "synagogue of Satan?" There were evidently Jews who denied that Christians were really God's chosen people. Christ here clearly states that Jews who have rejected him are no Jews at all. As Jesus said to the Jews when he fed the five thousand: "It is written in the prophets, 'And they shall all be taught by God.' Every one who has heard and learned from the Father comes to me" (John 6:45; cf. Isa. 54:13). The true Jew is one who recognizes Jesus as the Christ; those Jews who refuse, says Christ, will be compelled to bow at the feet of Gentile believers. What a shock this will be to unbelieving Israel, when the tables are turned (cf. Isa. 60:14; Phil. 2:11; Rev. 1:7). On that great day the unbelieving Jew will realize that "I [Christ] have loved you," or "I love you," i.e., the persecuted saints at Philadelphia and everywhere (cf. Isa. 43:4).

3. The Blessing (3:10-13). The reward for fidelity to Christ is his promise to keep them from the hour of trial or testing which is to come upon the entire world of men (*tēs oikoumenēs holēs*) (3:10; 12:9). This time of testing and distress is that of the "messianic woes" which are to precede the *parousia*. Will the Philadelphians also pass through these woes? Christ, by urging them to "hold fast" (3:11), seems to imply that they shall pass through it. John 17:15 is perhaps the best commentary on 3:10. Christ prays not that the believer be taken out of the world, but that they be kept from the Evil One.

"I am coming soon!" This is the keynote of the book. It is used to warn the unfaithful and to encourage the faithful. Here it is used in the latter sense. Since he is coming soon they are to "hold fast" and see that no one seizes their crown (3:12; cf. 2:10).

After the "hour of trial," Christ will come again and the conquerors will be made "a pillar in the temple of . . . God" (3:12). Since there will be no temple in the new Jerusalem (21:22), the promise is best interpreted spiritually, namely, that the believer will be inseparably united with God in the eschatological kingdom. The "pillar" also suggests the thought of fixedness — security, as the added words "never shall he go out of it [temple]" suggests (3:12; Jer. 1:18; Isa. 22:23; 56:5). In contrast to the physical insecurity of the earthquake region of Philadelphia is the promise of spiritual union (security) with God.

Christ says further that the "pillar" will have a threefold inscription: (1) "the name of my God," symbolizing complete commitment to God; (2) "the name of the city of my God, the new Jerusalem," symbolizing full citizenship in the eternal kingdom (cf. Phil. 3:20-21); and (3) "my own new name" symbolizing the full knowledge of Christ which will be ours on that day (cf. 19:12; I Cor. 13:12; I John 3:1-3).

G. The Letter to the Church at Laodicea (3:14-22)

1. The City of Laodicea. Laodicea was located on the banks of the Lycus River, "at the junction of several branches of the great trade-road from Ephesus to the East." It was the judicial center for that district, and an important commercial city with three important businesses: (1) banking; (2) manufacturing of woolen garments and rugs made from its famous glossy black wool; and (3) medicine. The god of health and healing, Asklepios, was worshiped at Laodicea and there was a "medical school" attached to his temple. In connection with her medical · products was a "Phrygian powder," a cure for weak eyes. These three factors undoubtedly are behind Christ's message to this church (3:17-18). The city was so wealthy, that after an earth-quake in A.D. 60, it refused Roman aid and rebuilt with her own funds.

Paul evidently knew this church and wrote it a letter (Col. 2:1; 4:13, 15, 16) which she was to send on to Colossae, and the church at Colossae was to send a letter which Paul had written her to Laodicea.

The inevitable apathy and stagnation which accompanies affluence evidently infiltrated the church at Laodicea. Although there was a sizeable Jewish population, they evidently did not cause any trouble for the Christians. Could the lukewarmness of the church have been responsible for the acceptance of the church by the non-Christians?

Christ speaks of himself as "the Amen," i.e., he is the personification of the truth. In Isaiah (65:16) God is called the God of truth (Hebrew spelling is *"amen"*). Christ as the Truth is the "faithful" and "true," or genuine, witness. "The beginning of God's creation" does not mean that Christ was the first created being, since he is referred to as eternal being (cf. John 1:1; Heb. 1:1-3).

2. The Condemnation (3:15-17). The Laodiceans receive no commendation from their Lord, but instead they receive the most scathing attack of all the churches. Yet, behind this attack is seen the loving concern of Christ (3:18 ff.). He condemns the church as a whole for its *lukewarmness* — it is neither cold nor hot. Their insipid condition gives Christ a sense of nausea. In an attempt to shock them out of their apathy and pride, he warns them by saying: So, therefore (*houtōs*), because you are in this insipid state, I will "spew you out of my mouth" (3:16).

47

That this is not a total rejection is clear from the admonition and invitation to renewal (3:18-22).

Why were the Laodiceans so lukewarm? The answer is seen in the prideful boasting of 3:17. They felt as though they had arrived, and this by their own efforts. Their boasting (3:17a) and Christ's indictment of them (3:17b-18) are all related to the industries of Laodicea. Rather than being spiritually rich, prosperous, and in need of nothing, Christ sees them as they truly are: "the wretched one, the pitiable one — poor, blind, and naked" (3:17b). The reference here is emphatic and it is to the spiritual condition of the believers, since the material wealth of the Christians at Laodicea is well known. The word for blindness (*tuphlos*) is often used of spiritual blindness and it probably is used here in anticipation of the figure of "eye-salve" (3:18; cf. Matt. 23:17). Christ is referring to the inability of the Laodiceans to see their spiritual poverty. Likewise, Christ uses the analogy of clothing with which they are familiar, and declares that they are spiritually naked (cf. Matt. 22:1-4).

3. The Call to Repentance (3:18-19). Therefore. As someone has said, when you read a "therefore" in Scripture, stop and see what it is there for! Here our Lord is saying, "therefore," i.e., in the light of your spiritually precarious position, "buy from me gold refined by fire that you may be rich." We are reminded of Peter's Epistle where he tells us that "we were ransomed . . . not with perishable things such as silver or gold, but with the precious blood of Christ" (I Peter 1:18-19; cf. Isa. 55:1 ff.). Also Christ says that they are to buy "white garments" to hide their nakedness. These garments probably symbolize the good works of the saints which issue from the regenerate life (cf. Matt. 22:11; Rev. 7:13-14).

And finally, they are to buy "salve" to anoint their eyes, that they may see. This probably refers to the anointing of the Holy Spirit who initiates us into Christian truth and guides us (cf. II Cor. 1:21-22; I John 1:21, 27; John 14:25; etc.).

That Christ has not completely cast his people off now becomes clear. Actually he says that he "loves" them, this is why he has spoken so severely to them (3:19). "The Lord disciplines him whom he loves" (Heb. 12:6a). It is only because he loves his proud, rebellious children that he "reproves" and "chastens" them.

Now Christ calls for an about face in the Laodicean attitude toward him. "Be zealous" is the present tense, i.e., begin to be zealous, on fire, and continue to be so. "Repent" is the aorist tense, repent now, make a once-for-all break with lukewarmness and false, unfounded pride.

4. The Blessing (3:20-22). Christ now addresses the church as a whole, but he appeals to the individuals for a personal response: "Behold, I stand at the door and knock; if *any one* hears my voice and opens the door, I will come in to him and eat with him, and he with me" (3:20). This great invitation is not to be restricted to the second coming of Christ, as some would insist, but it was an invitation to lukewarm Christians then and now, who long for a living, vital fellowship with Jesus Christ. If "any one" opens the door he will come in and sup with him (cf. John 10:9; Song of Sol. 5:2).

But intimate fellowship and communion is not all that is in store for him who will "be zealous and repent." The conqueror will have delegated to him by Christ a place by his throne in the kingdom (cf. Matt. 19:28; Luke 22:29-30). "He who has an ear, let him hear what the Spirit says to the churches" (3:22). The responsibility rests with the churches and the individuals in them, then and now!

IV. THE VISION IN HEAVEN (4:1–5:14)

John has already revealed the glorious vision of the Son of Man moving in the midst of the churches (1:12-20). He presented a picture of the church in Christ's letters to the seven churches. This is what was and is (1:19). Now he is to reveal what shall be. "The fulfillment of God's purposes concerning his kingdom is near. The vision here opened, consisting of two inseparably connected parts, Chapters 4 and 5, furnishes the foundation and assurance of all that follows — God enthroned over all in eternal majesty and power, Chapter 4; giving over the book of his will to Christ, the Lamb, the Revealer, and Fulfiller, Chapter 5. These are the supreme 'things that are,' out of which the 'things that are to come to pass' must flow certainly and completely in spite of the powers of evil" (Beckwith).

This vision of God and Christ is foundational, for it is from these which present God as Creator and Lord of history, and Christ as an all powerful and omniscient Redeemer, i.e., conqueror of death, that John and the church derive strength to face the future assured of victory.

A. The Vision of God the Creator (4:1-11)

1. The Call to Heaven (4:1-2a). "After this I looked." The phrase recurs several times (7:1; 7:9; 15:5; 18:1; cf. 19:1), but it does not indicate an exact chronology of events. After receiving the messages for the "seven churches," John sees the heavens opening as a door before him (cf. Ezek. 1:1; Acts 7:56; 10:11). From heaven John heard the same voice which spoke to him earlier (1:10) calling him into heaven: "Come up hither, and I will show you what must take place after this." The "after this" is revealed when Christ breaks the seals of the scroll (6:1).

"At once I was in the Spirit." Although the language seems to imply the beginning of ecstasy, in reality it is a continuation of the same ecstatic experience referred to earlier (cf. 1:10; Ezek. 11:5).

2. God Enthroned and Surrounded by Twenty-four Elders (4:2b-6a). The first thing that catches John's eye is the throne on which God is seated (4:2b). He does not actually see God; instead he sees his glory which he endeavors to describe (4:3).

The important point to lay hold of is that Almighty God is enthroned in heaven — he is in control.

Although Isaiah (6:1-8), Ezekiel (1:1-28), Daniel (7:1-28), and I Kings (22:19) provide the background for this throne vision, John himself, inspired by the Holy Spirit, is responsible for this majestic description.

The brilliance and beauty of the throne vision is conveyed by the use of precious stones and the rainbow (4:3).

The glory of God appearing as "jasper" suggests translucence — brightness, probably symbolizing the holiness of God. The "fiery-red sardis," or "carnelian," suggests the wrath of God, while the "emerald rainbow" "is thought to be the rock crystal which shows a rainbow of prismatic colors." Although in Ezekiel the bow suggests the splendor of God, it is best to see here the covenant promise of God to Noah never to destroy the earth with water (Gen. 9:8 ff.). Note it is the "emerald rainbow" which surrounds the throne and hides the full brightness of God's glory from John's view.

The "twenty-four elders" who are seated on thrones surrounding God's throne are generally understood to symbolize the people of God (4:4). Twelve elders symbolize the patriarchs of "old Israel," and twelve elders symbolize the Apostles and the "new Israel" of God. The "white garments" symbolize purity and victory, and the "golden crown" the fact that they are privileged to reign with God.

Verse 5 is reminiscent of Exodus 19:16. The "flashes of lightning" and the "voices" (Gk. "claps of thunder") signify God's awe-inspiring majesty and power. The "seven torches of fire" are the "seven spirits of God," or the Holy Spirit. The pavement of God's throne room was like a "sea of glass." This suggests the waters above the firmament, and symbolizes God's transcendance (4:6; cf. Exod. 24:10; Ezek. 1:26; Gen. 1:7).

3. The Four Living Creatures and the Elders Praise God the Creator (4:6b-11). "Four living creatures" surround the throne of God, one on each side. The background for this is primarily Ezekiel 1:4 ff. and Isaiah 6:2 f. These four creatures are significantly different from those in Ezekiel. In Ezekiel they each have four faces, here only one; in Ezekiel they have wheels full of eyes, but here the creatures have eyes "in front and behind" (4:6b). R. H. Charles believes these four creatures are cherubim (Ezek. 1:4 ff.), while Beckwith, who believes the twenty-four elders are "angelic beings," believes these four living creatures are "the highest order of angelic beings, who apparently stand nearest the throne." These four creatures who represent all the

51

creatures of the earth, continually praise and magnify the Eternal God — "who was and is and is to come!" (4:8). The notion of Irenaeus that the four creatures symbolize the four Gospels is without foundation. The fact that these creatures are "full of eyes all around and within" suggests that they can see all. The six wings remind us of the cherubim in Isaiah (6:2-3).

Whenever the "four living creatures" sing their song of praise, giving "glory and honor and thanks" to God (4:9), then the twenty-four elders are moved to prostrate themselves before Jehovah's throne, and cast down their crowns, and join in praising him who alone is worthy "to receive glory and honor and power" because he is creator and sustainer of the universe (4:10-11).

The reader will probably recognize immediately that these words and those from Isaiah's vision in the temple form the background for the familiar hymn "Holy, Holy, Holy" (4:8b-11; Isa. 6:3).

B. The Vision of Christ the Redeemer (5:1-14)

1. The Sealed Scroll in God's Right Hand (5:1-5). John now moves on to describe the scroll "sealed with seven seals" (5:1). This roll contains the revelations of God for the future of the world and the church. Zahn tells us that "seven seals" are used to seal up testaments or wills, so here we have God's revelation of the future. That which has been concealed is about to be revealed (cf. Isa. 29:11; Dan. 8:26).

A "strong," or "mighty angel," now appears and cries with a "loud voice" for one who was "worthy (*axios*) to open the scroll and break its seal" (5:2). Worthy, not in the sense of strong, but in the sense of status and ability — one who can execute God's purposes as they are revealed. "Worthiness and ability are here identical," hence, he was able (*edunato*) (5:3). The angel must be strong because his cry must extend into the three spheres of the world — heavens, earth, and Hades (5:3; cf. Phil. 2:10; Exod. 20:4).

Since no one responded to the angel's call, it looked as though the promise of 4:1 would not be fulfilled. Therefore, John wept.

Then, as John despaired, one of the elders brought the good news that One had been found (5:5). He is none other than "the Lion of the tribe of Judah" (cf. Gen. 49:9), "The Root of David" (cf. Isa. 11:1, 10; Matt. 1:1), who is worthy and will open the scroll and its seals. He was proven worthy because he "has conquered" (*enikēsen*) — conquered sin and Satan (cf. 3:21; Heb. 2:14). Jesus the Christ (Messiah) has fulfilled the

Old Testament hope by his crucial victory over Satan at the cross, and soon he will complete his victory at his second coming.

2. The Adoration of the Lamb (5:6-14). In the midst of the throne John sees a "Lamb standing, as though it had been slain" (5:6). He was told that "the Lion of the tribe of Judah" was found, but when he looked he saw a "Lamb." Here the Davidic and Suffering Servant concepts of the Messiah are fused — the Messiah of David is the Lamb of God who took away the sins of the world (cf. Isa. 11:1, 10; 53:7; John 1:29; I Cor. 5:7b). The Lamb is described as *almighty* and *omniscient*. These attributes are conveyed by the "seven horns" and the "seven eyes which are the seven spirits of God sent out into all the earth" (5:6). "Horn" is a common Biblical symbol of power, and here the number seven suggests the completeness, or perfection, of his power. The "seven eyes which are the seven spirits of God" were attributed to Jehovah (Zech. 4:10b), but here they suggest Christ's omniscience, and the Holy Spirit which he and the Father sent into the world (cf. John 16:7).

When the Lamb took the scroll from God's hand, then the four living creatures and the twenty-four elders fell down before the Lamb. Besides a harp, they held a "golden bowl full of incense, which are the prayers of the saints" (5:7-8). The angelic character of the elders is confirmed here by the fact that they bring the prayers of the saints before the throne.

The "new song" is new because of the *new theme* (cf. Ps. 33:3; 40:3; 96:1). The theme is the Lamb who was slain, providing a ransom by his blood (5:9). The Old Testament teaches that without the shedding of blood there is no remission of sins (cf. Lev. 17:11). All praise to the Lamb, then, for he has ransomed us by his blood (cf. Rev. 1:5b; Heb. 9:12; Mark 10:45). This redemption was not for the Jew only, but for the Gentile — for those of "every tribe and tongue and people and nation." But not only has he "ransomed" men from sin's bondage, he also "*has made* them a kingdom and priests to our God and they shall reign on earth" (5:10). "Here we have three particulars: (1) Those who are bought to be God's own, are made into a kingdom, viz., God's; (2) They are made into priests; (3) They are invested with kingly power" (Scott). That we are a "royal priesthood" now is true (I Peter 2:9), but here the reference is to the millennial reign of the saints — not just the martyred saints of the first century, but of all the saints (cf. 20:4-6).

After this "new song," an innumerable host of angels who surround God, the Lamb, and the others, join in a peon of praise to the Lamb for what he has wrought by his death, and for other qualities which he possesses (5:12). "The analogy of other doxologies, e.g., 1:6, 4:11; 7:12, shows that the meaning here is not that Christ is worthy to receive what God has given him, might, etc., but as in 4:11 to receive adoration for the might, etc., which he possesses" (Beckwith). Then, every creature in all of creation will join in praising God and the Lamb (5:13).

To this angelic chorus the "four living creatures" say "Amen," and the elders prostrate themselves and worship the Lamb (5:14).

V. THE VISION OF THE SEVEN SEALS (6:1–8:5)

Beginning with the seven seals, John shares with us the vision he received of things that are to take place "hereafter." The reader will note a similarity between the seven woes here and the woes of our Lord in his eschatological discourse in Luke (21:9-12). In Luke's account the "earthquake is third," but in John's revelation the earthquake is the last messianic woe, marking the passing of the old aeon and presaging the Messianic Age (8:5; 11:13; 16:18).

There are "seven seals" (followed by seven trumpets and seven bowls) to symbolize the complete judgment of God against evil (cf. Lev. 26:18, 21, 24, 28). The intensity of God's judgment increases with each cycle of seven woes, until with the seven bowls comes the complete judgment of God against evil. Between the sixth and seventh woe of the first two cycles, however, an interlude is presented which assures the suffering saints ultimate victory (7:1-17; 10:1–11:14).

As all prophecy has a short range and a long range application, so John's visions relate to his day and to some future day — the consummation of this age and the dawn of the new.

A. The First Seal (6:1-2)

The background for the first four woes (seals) is Zechariah (6:1 ff.), but John's treatment is peculiar to this new revelation. Again, caution must be exercised and we must reject the temptation to read Old Testament meaning into this new revelation. God did something *new* in Christ, and we must look for what he is saying in this new revelation.

When the first seal is opened, one of the four living creatures calls "with a voice of thunder," loud and clear, "Come." The call to "come" was not to John, for he was already in heaven (4:1), but it was to the horse and its rider. Note the call to "come" is omitted from the last three woes.

The "white horse" and the rider with a "bow" has been interpreted as referring to: (1) the victorious coming of Christ (cf. 19:11 ff.); or (2) the victorious spread of the gospel which must precede his coming (Mark 13:10); or (3) the victorious conquest, not of Christ, but of evil here personified. The latter interpretation is preferred for several reasons: (1) Christ is opening the seals and therefore would not be a rider, too; (2) the four horsemen are a unity all symbolizing the spread of evil; (3) the triumph of God in Christ does not come until the long series of God's judgments are unfolded and the balance of the vision takes place. The "white horse" may symbolize victory, either good or evil, and in this place, evil (Moffatt, Swete, Bengel, etc.).

Some identify the horseman with the bow to whom a crown is given with the Parthians, Rome's perennial foe from the east. This may well be one identification, but it does not exhaust its meaning. At any rate, this power goes forth "conquering" (has already conquered), and "to conquer" (to make future conquests) (6:2). For the three fold conquest of sword, famine and pestilence see Jeremiah 15:2; 21:7; 29:17, and Ezekiel 14:12-21 which adds "beasts."

B.   The Second Seal (6:3-4)

This rider with a great sword upon a "bright red" horse is commissioned to remove peace from the earth. He symbolizes internal turmoil, civil war, and perhaps international conflict. The "red" color probably symbolizes the slaughter which accompanies war.

C.   The Third Seal (6:5-6)

The "black horse" with a rider holding a "balance" in his hand symbolizes famine — scarcity of food. During the reign of Domitian, when this Apocalypse was written, there was a famine in the Empire. There was a severe scarcity of grain, so that a quart of grain, which was the daily consumption of a man, was sold for a *denarius*, the daily wage of a laborer (cf. Matt. 20:2). This resulted in severe privations for his family — possibly starvation. Wine and oil, however, were not harmed; there was an abundance of these.

D.   The Fourth Seal (6:6-8)

The last horse is "pale," or "greenish-grey;" the Greek is *chlōros* from which we get our word "chlorine." He symbolizes death as wrought by the fourfold instrumentalities mentioned: sword, famine, pestilence and wild beasts (6:8; cf. Ezek. 5:12; 14:21; 16:12). Verse 8 is not merely a summary of the second and third woes, but is a new one, more inclusive (Charles). Although Christ vanquished death and Hades (1:18), those who reject him are subject both to the pestilences mentioned, and death and Hades (6:8). The Septuagint (LXX) uses "death" (*thanatos*) to translate the Hebrew "pestilence" (*dever*) (cf. Jer. 14:12; 24:10; Lev. 26:25); that is the meaning here, since a special form of death is meant, as shown by the connection with the other substantives (Beckwith).

E. The Fifth Seal (6:9-11)

John's cycles of sevens are often divided into two groups; we had four horses dealing with the messianic woes on earth, now we have three signs of a different nature. The fifth seal relates the blessed state of the martyred saints as they await the end.

The souls of the martyrs are "under the altar" (6:9). It is probably the altar of burnt-offering and not the altar of incense which the author has in mind in this heavenly temple of God. The concept of heaven as God's temple is common in the Apocalypse and the Old Testament (cf. 11:19; 14:15, 17; 15:5, 8; Ps. 18:6; Hab. 2:20, etc.). According to Hebrew customs, the blood of the sacrificial victim was poured out at the base of the altar of burnt-offering (Lev. 4:7). So in the Christian community, the thought probably is that the blood of the martyrs was poured out as a sacrificial offering to God (cf. Phil. 2:17; II Tim. 4:6). Christians probably went on to develop the idea that the souls of the martyrs were safe and secure under the altar of burnt-offering in heaven. The rabbis held such a view in the second century.

These souls were those who were slain because of their faithfulness to the "Word of God and for the witness they had borne," i.e., "even for the testimony borne by Jesus" is what is intended. The "and" (*kai*) is epexegetical, or explanatory, "even." It is the witness of Christ which they had received and faithfully kept.

The anguished prayer for revenge is frequently contrasted by commentators with Christ's and Stephen's dying prayers for the forgiveness of their enemies (Luke 23:32; Acts 7:60), and it is said that the martyr's cry is "sub-Christian." What is being overlooked is that whenever we pray to God for deliverance from a foe in times of crisis we are unwittingly praying for the judgment of our foes (cf. Luke 18:7-8). It is difficult for Americans who have never suffered as Christians did in the early centuries, nor as many do in some parts of the world today, to truly empathize with the martyred saints.

In answer to their query, "How long?" the martyred saints are given a "white robe," symbolizing victory and immortality to be bestowed upon them at the first resurrection, and then they are told to wait until the fixed number of martyrs is complete. Apocalyptic writers like John were fully persuaded that God was sovereign and this shows itself in the idea here of a "fixed number" to be martyred before the "fixed time" of the end comes.

F. The Sixth Seal (6:12-17)

After the "breather" of the fifth seal, Christ opens the sixth seal which reveals in dreadful symbolism familiar to Old Testament ·Apocalyptic prophecy, those plagues belonging to the "forerunners of the last calamities." The important point John is trying to convey is that in the last days life will become so unbearable that men will cry out for death to overtake them. For the background for the picture of cosmic unheaval and catastrophe associated with the "end-time" see the Old Testament references to: "earthquakes" (cf. Ezek. 38:19 f.; Isa. 2:19; Hag. 2:6); "sun" blackened and "moon like blood (cf. Joel 2:31; Ezek. 32:7); "stars" falling like fig leaves in a winter gale (cf. Isa. 34:4; Nah. 3:12) the "sky vanish like a scroll" (cf. Isa. 34:4); "mountains" and "islands" moved (cf. Ps. 114:4; Jer. 4:24). When these catastrophes come, then all manner of men, from the mightiest to lowliest, shall hide in the "caves" and "among the rocks" and call for them to fall upon them and hide them from the face of God and the wrath of the Christ (6:15-16; cf. Isa. 2:10, 19; Luke 23:30; Hos. 10:8). *The Great Day of Wrath has come,* that spoken of in Joel (2:11, 31b), Nahum (1:6), and Malachi (3:2). That day will be so fierce, none of the ungodly will be able to endure it. The symbolism employed here is that, *symbolism,* but the event described is anticipated as *real.* Judgment is sure and certain, and it will be catastrophic in its effect. God and the Lamb shall execute righteous judgment (cf. 5:5; 6:10).

G. The Interlude, the Saints Sealed (7:1-17)

As is the custom of the apocalyptist, when the picture looks blackest, he injects a vision which lifts the suffering saints from despair to hope. We would naturally expect the end to come after that frightful sixth plague, but instead we have an interlude. John sees two visions which point to the certain triumph of the church, the people of God (7:1-8, 9-17). The first vision views the church on earth. God pledges to protect her through all the trials which may befall her. The second vision anticipates the final triumph of Christ and the saints when full salvation becomes a reality. The first vision promises salvation; and in the second vision, it is realized.

1. The Sealing of God's Servants (7:1-8). "After this" marks a logical transition, and not a chronological one. John sees

"four angels standing at the four corners of the earth, holding back the four winds of the earth" (7:1). The Jews believed that angels were in charge of the elements. "The figure of the *four* winds as destructive agencies, or as connected with portents is a familiar one (cf. Jer. 49:36; Dan. 7:2; Zech. 6:5)" (Beckwith). Here the four angels hold back the four winds, symbolizing the staying of God's judgment until the saints are sealed (7:3).

A fifth angel ascends from the rising of the sun (cf. Ezek. 43:4). This angel has the seal of the Living God upon him. He calls to the four angels who have the power to harm the earth and sea and tells them not to unleash the evil winds until the servants of God are sealed upon their foreheads (7:3). The idea of sealing God's faithful children goes back to Ezekiel (9:4; cf. Song of Sol. 15:8).

Here it is not merely the martyrs who are sealed, but *all* the servants of God. The seal could be a mark of authentication (Rom. 4:11), or a means of security (Rev. 5:1; 20:3). In 7:3 both ideas are included. In contrast to the mark of the Beast (13:16 f.), this seal on the believer authenticates him as a true believer. But the primary purpose of the seal here, as in Ezekiel, "is a token or pledge of security." But from what are the saints being preserved? Most interpreters agree they are being secured against the multitudinous plagues which are to come upon men with the breaking of the seventh seal.

Just what the seal is, we cannot say. Some have suggested "the name of Jehovah," and others "Baptism."

The number of the sealed is 144,000 out of every tribe in Israel (7:4). The number is arrived at by squaring twelve and multiplying it a thousandfold. The early Christians believed that they were the members of the new Israel of God, his chosen people, as we shall readily see. Many interpretations have been suggested for the 144,000: (1) they are Jewish Christians, while the innumerable multitude of 7:9-10 are all the believers, including Jews; (2) they are the "chosen remnant" of Israel who have accepted Jesus as the Messiah — righteous Jews only, who are to be delivered from the coming distresses; (3) they are the Israelites who will eventually be grafted into the olive tree — the true Israel of God — a remnant of each tribe which will be converted in the end; (4) they are a small select group chosen out of the church because of their purity (14:4).

The interpretation which is supported by the majority of Biblical scholarship of all schools is that the 144,000 symbolize

the whole body of Christ, the church, both Jew and Gentile.
Paul refers to the church as the true Israel, and to Christians as
true Jews (cf. Rom. 2:28-29; Gal. 3:29; 6:16; Phil. 3:3). James
and Peter referred to Christians as "the twelve tribes" (James
1:1; I Peter 1:1; 2:9). Especially in this Apocalypse is the
Jewish symbolism used. Christians are the true Jews of God's
assembly (synagogue) (2:9; 3:9). The city of the church
triumphant is called the "new Jerusalem" and the names of the
"twelve tribes" are inscribed on the gates of the city (20:9; 21:
2, 12). That the author intended to symbolize the entire believing community (church) is seen in 14:1 where the 144,000
are on Mt. Zion with the Lamb.

Twelve thousand are chosen from every tribe, except Dan
(7:5-8). John arranges the tribes uniquely. Judah, the messianic tribe from which our Lord is descended, is rightly listed
first. Iranaeus interpreted Jeremiah 8:16 to suggest that Dan
was omitted because it was believed that the Antichrist was to
come from his tribe (cf. Testament of Dan 5:6). In order to
make up for his omission Joseph is used along with Manasseh.

2. The Redeemed before the Throne (7:9-17). Thus in this
vision (7:1-8) we see the church militant secured by God during
the terrible days of distress through which the world is to pass.
John now relates another vision, an anticipating one, which
pictures the church triumphant around the throne, together
with all the heavenly hosts, worshipping God and the Lamb.
This preview of the final blessed state is given to encourage the
church during the critical times through which it was, and
would be, passing.

a. The Innumerable Multitude (7:9-12). The "great multitude which no man could number" is drawn from every nation
on the face of the earth (7:9; cf. Mark 13:10; Matt. 28:19-20).
This multitude is the same as the 144,000 (7:7; 14:1). Here
they stand "clothed in white robes," a sign of their resurrection
glory, with "palm branches in their hands," a sign of victory
and rejoicing after battle (cf. John 12:13). In their victory song
they ascribe the work of salvation to God and the Lamb (7:
10, 12; 19:1; cf. Ps. 3:8). No sooner does the redeemed
multitude ascribe glory to God and the Lamb, than the angelic
hosts, the four living creatures and the elders all fall on their
faces before the throne and affirm the song of the multitude
with a hearty "Amen" (7:11-12a). Then they add their own
"seven-fold doxology" in which they glorify God for this great
salvation (7:12; cf. Luke 15:10).

b. The Interpretation of the Vision (7:13-14). John is then confronted by one of the elders who asks him the meaning of this glorious vision he has just seen (7:13). The question is proposed not for the elder's benefit, but for John's. John's reply, "Sir, you know," really means, "Sir, I don't know, won't you tell me?" (7:14). The reply of the elder has been called a "Martyr's Hymn" in four strophes (7:14-17).

"The great tribulation" in mind here is that which takes place in *the last days,* the time of trouble before the parousia which John expected momentarily. Those in "white robes" are those who have washed them "in the blood of the Lamb" (7:14). All believers are in view here, not just martyrs. To be washed in the blood of the Lamb symbolizes the renewal of the believer through the act of regeneration and sanctification (cf. 22:14; 1:5; I John 1:7; Titus 3:5-6; Heb. 9:14). The idea of washing away sin and putting on righteousness is a familiar one (cf. Isa. 1:18 f.).

Because they have experienced regeneration in Christ, the second strophe points up to specific blessings (7:15). First of all they "serve him day and night in the temple." The Greek word for serve is *latreuousin* which "denotes here the ritual service in the temple; cf. Heb. 8:5" (Love). However, it is sound exposition to make the point that the believer will be blessed with a life of continued service and growth in the eternal kingdom. The idea of "saints" sitting around idle in heaven is not one the Apocalypse advocates. A second blessing will be that of having God "shelter them with his presence." The translation here retains the idea of God's "shekinah glory" overshadowing his people as he did in Israel around the tabernacle and temple (cf. Lev. 16:2; Rev. 21:3; John 1:14).

The third strophe assures the saints that they will not have any unfulfilled desires (7:16; cf. John 4:14; Isa. 49:10), nor will they have occasion to fear the heat, probably the scorching, suffocating wind known as the "sirocco" (Ps. 121:6).

In the final strophe, the saints are promised that the Lamb, who was slain and came to life again, will be their shepherd (cf. John 10:11; Ps. 23; Ezek. 34:23). Again he promises that their innermost needs will be met, for the Lamb shall lead them "to springs of living water" (cf. John 4:14; Rev. 21:6; 22:1, 17).

And finally he says to these Christians, who undoubtedly have suffered untold agony, that "God shall wipe away every tear from their eyes." What great consolation these verses must have brought to the ears of God's people then, and still do today.

H. The Seventh Seal (8:1-5)

1. The Seventh Seal Opened (8:1-2). The Lamb, after granting the saints a foretaste of glory, opens the seventh seal. Following this there is silence in heaven for about "half an hour" (8:1). Beasley-Murray relates a Jewish tradition which states that the angels of the fifth heaven "sing praises to God at night but keep silent by day so that the praises of Israel might be heard." He goes on to suggest, as other commentators do also, that the dramatic pause before the blowing of the seven trumpets was for the express purpose of giving time for the prayers of Christians to be carried to the throne. Some have suggested the pause occurs as the heavenly host awaits the events which will now come upon the earth.

The "seven angels" who stand before God are believed to be the "angels of his presence": Michael, Gabriel, Raphael, Uriel, Raguel, Sariel, and Remiel. The presence of "el," one of the names for God, indicates their close association with God (cf. Luke 1:19; Tobit 12:15). Each angel is given a trumpet which is connected with the next cycle of seven woes or plagues. Trumpets are frequently associated with eschatological messages, and here, as elsewhere, they are used to announce the impending judgment of God (8:2; cf. Isa. 27:13; Joel 2:1; Matt. 24:31; I Cor. 15:52; I Thess. 4:16).

2. The Incense and the Prayers of the Saints (8:3-5). The seven angels did not blow their trumpets immediately; instead, during this pause, the prayers of the saints which were mingled with incense are wafted into God's presence (8:3). "This prelude to the seven trumpet-blasts given in these verses expresses the familiar thought, the agency of the prayers of the saints in bringing in the judgment of the world and the fulfillment of the kingdom; see 6:9 f." (Beckwith). The prayers here referred to are those of the saints on earth crying to God for deliverance.

The other angel (8:3) stands before the altar, the golden altar of incense, with a golden censer. "Much" incense was given the angel to mingle with the prayers of the saints because of the large volume of intercessory prayers being made. Note the incense is mingled *with* the prayers of the saints. Beasley-Murray says that incense helps to make the prayers more acceptable to God. There is no thought of mediatorial angels here; the prayers rise directly to God.

When the prayers of the saints reach the throne of God (8:4), God answers. The angel "took the censer and filled it with fire from the altar and threw it on the earth" (8:5a). The casting of the fire upon the earth symbolizes the impending wrath and judgment of God in response to the intercession of the saints, as the signs which follow indicate (8:5b).

Signs also follow the seventh trumpet (11:19) and the seventh bowl (16:18). Ezekiel (10:4) records a somewhat parallel scene in which live coals are scattered over Jerusalem as a symbol of God's judgment. Note how the prophet John continually reassures the suffering saints of the inevitability of the final triumph.

VI. THE VISION OF THE SEVEN TRUMPETS (8:6–11:19)

We now come to a consideration of the message of the vision of the seven trumpets. These are divided into four and three, as were the seven seals. The first four bring judgment primarily upon the *natural* world — "earth, sea, rivers and fountains, and luminaries," while the last three are directed specifically upon men. The background for these plagues is the Exodus plagues.

It should be noted that these trumpet plagues are more severe than those of the seals, and we shall see that those of the bowls are the most severe of all. In the first series (seals) the phenomena is ordinary and natural. In the second series (trumpets) a supernatural element is added, and the suffering is more intense and widespread. In the third series (bowls) God's wrath is more severe than in the second series, thereby causing man's hostility and rebellion against God to be greater. Note also that there is an interlude of encouragement to the saints between the sixth and seventh trumpet.

A. The First Trumpet (8:7)

The first trumpet produces a plague of "hail and fire mixed with blood" which affects a third of the earth, trees, and grass (8:7). For the Old Testament background for "hail" see Exodus 9:33 ff.; "blood," see 7:17 ff.; and "fire and blood," see Joel 2:30. Note that only one-third of the grass is destroyed (8:7; cf. 9:4; 16:2).

B. The Second Trumpet (8:8-9)

We are reminded here of the Exodus plagues in which one-third of the Nile was turned to blood, only here it is one-third of the sea which turns to blood after "something like a great mountain, burning with fire, was thrown into the sea" (8:8; cf. Exod. 7:17 ff.). As a result of this burning mass being cast into the sea one-third of the ships and fish are destroyed. There are kindred ideas in some of the literature of the Pseudepigrapha in which the burning mass was rebellious fallen angels, but there is no suggestion of that here (I Enoch 18:13; 21:3; Sibylline Oracles V. 158).

C. The Third Trumpet (8:10-11)

The "great star" blazing like a torch which falls from heaven and pollutes one-third of the rivers and fountains of water was named *Wormwood* (8:10-11a). Stars symbolize angels. The fact that "many men" die from the bitter water indicates that the water did not *literally* become wormwood (8:11b). This plague is like that of Marah in reverse (Exod. 13:23). The corruption of drinking water reminds us of the first Egyptian plague, but here wormwood is the means used. Wormwood symbolizes divine punishment, as Jeremiah's words indicate: "I will feed this people with wormwood, and give them poisonous water to drink" (Jer. 9:15; cf. 23:15; Lam. 3:15, 19).

D. The Fourth Trumpet (8:12)

The background for the fourth plague which affects the luminaries of the heavens is the Egyptian plague of darkness (Exod. 10:21; cf. Isa. 13:10; Joel 2:31; Amos 8:9). This plague is not designed to destroy, but only to warn men of the wrath to come.

E. The Fifth Trumpet (8:13—9:11)

Before the next three trumpets are blown an eagle comes to warn the wicked inhabitants of the earth of the severity of the last three trumpets. That the wicked of the earth are intended, see 9:4, 20. This verse (8:13) marks the transition from the first four trumpets to the last three.

The fifth trumpet introduces a plague of demonic locusts. John sees a "star fallen from heaven to earth" (9:1a). That this "star" symbolizes an angel employed by God for a specific task, and *not* Satan himself, is clear because Satan is nowhere in Scripture employed by God (cf. 20:1). There are numerous references in canonical and apocryphal literature to stars symbolizing fallen, rebellious angels, but the star in 9:1 is not a demon (cf. I Enoch 21:6; 90:24; 18:15 f.; Jude 13). This angel is given a key to the bottomless pit which he opens, and from it arises a dense smoke which darkens the sun and air (9:1b-2; cf. Gen. 19:28; Exod. 19:18; Joel 2:10). The "bottomless pit" is a provisional place of punishment for Satan until the end when he is thrown into the "lake of fire" (20:1-3, 10). From the smoke come swarms of locusts which are given power to harm like scorpions, not nature, but those evil and rebellious men who have not the seal of God upon their foreheads (9:3-4). These locusts represent demonic forces unleashed against wicked men. They are permitted to torture them for five months, but not to kill them (9:5a).

The life span of a scorpion was five months (spring and summer). Scorpions do not kill, but they do make one deathly sick. To people familiar with locust plagues and scorpions as

65

John's readers were, the imagery would convey a frightening message of impending suffering. Indeed, so severe will be the torment that men will long for death, but death will not overtake them (9:5).

The Old Testament background for this picture is Joel 2:1-11, where the Day of the Lord is described under the figure of a devastating plague of locusts. In Joel the judgment is directed against Israel, but here it is directed against the enemies of God. The reader should study the above passage in Joel in connection with this fifth trumpet plague and first woe. The symbolism employed by John in his vision is different from that in Joel, but its message is no less frightening. Both point to the day of wrath and judgment. The appearance of these locusts were "like horses arrayed for battle" (9:7a). "There is an Arab saying often quoted in illustration of our passage to the effect that the locust has a head like a horse, a breast like a lion, feet like a camel, a body like a serpent, and antennae like the hair of a maiden" (Beckwith). Interestingly, he also calls attention to the fact that the similarity between the two is conveyed in the Italian words for "locust," *cavalletta,* and "horse," *cavallo.*

"On their heads were what looked like crowns of gold" and "their faces were like human faces" (9:7). This is designed to convey the idea that these are not ordinary locusts, but instead, symbolic representations of the demonic forces of evil. The "hair like a woman's hair" probably refers to their long antennae (9:8a), while their lion-like teeth refer to "the voracity of the locusts in devouring vegetation" (9:8a). "The scales like iron breastplates" might suggest the breast-shield of the war-horse (9:9a). "The noise of their wings was like the noise of many chariots with horses rushing into battle." This is just like the description in Joel of the hosts of chariots rushing into battle (Joel 2:5). The power of the locusts to inflict punishment is in the scorpion-like tails of these demonic locusts because they are directing their hostility against men and not vegetation (9:10). The leader of these demonic forces is not Satan, but an angel who presides over the bottomless pit. *Abaddōn,* the Hebrew name of the angel, means "destruction" or the "place of destruction." Beckwith says that *Abaddōn* "becomes a proper name equivalent to Sheol, Hades (e.g., Job 26:6; Prov. 15:11); it is such in cases where personification is intended (e.g., Job 28:22), as Death and Hades are personified in our book cf. 6:8." John translates the angel's name from the Hebrew *Abaddōn* into Greek, *Apollyōn, Destroyer.*

We have seen in the above scene that the judgment of God

has shifted from the world of nature to the world of wicked men. God has permitted these demonic forces of hell, the "bottomless pit," with which man in his rebellion against God has been in league, to vent their diabolic powers against him.

F. The Sixth Trumpet (9:12-21)

John tells us that the first woe is past and that two more are coming (9:12).

With the sixth trumpet blast a voice cries out "from the four horns of the golden altar before God" (9:13). It was from this altar that the prayers of the saints, mingled with incense, were wafted to the throne of God (8:4-5). Now God is answering their prayers in this and the other plagues. The voice commands the sixth angelic trumpeter to "release the four angels who are at the great river *Euphrates*," (9:14; cf. 7:1-3). These four angels were to lead the devastating armies of 200,000,000 cavalry from beyond the Euphrates to kill one third of mankind (9:15).

Large devastating armies from the region *north* of Israel, from around the great river Euphrates are closely associated in prophecy with the final conflict. There are numerous references in prophetic literature to fierce armies of destruction (cf. Ezek. 38—39; Isa. 5:26 ff.; Jer. 1·14 ff.; 6:22 f.; Joel 3:9 ff.; Zech. 14:2). A prominent part of these armies is always the horse (cf. Isa. 5:28; Jer. 4:13; Ezek. 26:7, 10; Hab. 1:8). In Old Testament times, the prophets predicted that powers from beyond the Euphrates would come upon Israel in judgment, but now John sees them coming upon the enemy of the "new Israel" — the Christian community. By stating that the four angels were restrained until a precise moment points up the Apostle's conviction that God is in control and that he has planned a precise time for each event (9:15).

The scene now switches to the large army of cavalrymen of 200,000,000 (9:16). Note that it is the horses which actually wreak the destruction and not the riders (9:17-19). The "riders" only wear defensive armor — breast-plates (9:17). It was the "fire and smoke and sulphur" issuing from the horses' mouths which actually destroyed one third of the human race. John emphasizes that "the power of the horses was in their mouths, and in their tails," thereby joining this sixth plague with the fifth. In the fifth the scorpion-like tail of the locust only wounded, but in the sixth we still have the continued torture by the tails of the horses which are like serpents' heads, but there is the added judgment of the destruction of one third of mankind (9:19).

The purpose of the plagues was redemptive, however, and not merely punative (cf. Amos 4:6-11). John tells us that "the rest" of mankind who survived the slaughter did not repent. The two things they refused to repent of were idolatry and immorality (9:20-21). When men reject or forsake the one true God, they not only turn to idolatry, but also to all manner of immoral practices. True religion and ethical living are inseparable (cf. Jer. 2:13; Isa. 1:2 ff.; Rom. 1:18-32; etc.).

G. The Interlude of the Little Scroll and the Temple and the Witnesses (10:1—11:13)

John has now moved from heaven (4:1) to earth (10:1). As is his custom, the author pauses to share a vision designed to encourage and sustain the saints in their witness. The interlude is longer than the one between the sixth and seventh seal, and it is divided into two parts: one is directed especially to the prophet John (10:1-11), while the other is addressed to the persecuted church (11:1-13).

1. The Announcement of the Imminence of the End (10:1-7). Since the angel descended from heaven to earth (10:1) and John later receives the scroll from his hand (10:8-9), we conclude that the prophet is now upon earth. The new mighty angel is arrayed in a "cloud" which is probably associated with his mission of judgment. The description of the angel with "the rainbow over his head, and his face . . . like the sun, and his legs like pillars of fire" all suggest the appearance of heavenly glory, but we should not identify this angel with Christ (10:1). The oath the angel takes in 10:6 precludes this identification.

When the angel comes to earth he has a "little scroll *open* in his hand" (10:2a). This "little scroll" is to be distinguished from the one in God's hand which was sealed (5:1). The angel rests one of his feet upon the sea and the other upon the land, thereby symbolizing that the message of the little open scroll is for the entire world (10:3).

The angel then calls out with a *loud* voice, like a lion roaring. After this, "seven thunders sounded" (10:3; cf. Ps. 29), and each speaks a definite message to John; but when he moves to record them he is forbidden to do so by "a voice from heaven" which tells him to "seal up what the seven thunders have said, and do not write it down" (10:4). The voice from heaven was probably that of God or Christ (cf. 1:11, 19; John 12:28). Because the end was near, and because of the evident inappropriateness of this personal revelation through the seven thunders, and the importance of the rest of the vision, John is told not to record the vision.

The angel with the little scroll, with hands lifted toward heaven, then makes a fourfold vow in the name of the *Eternal Creator* that after the seventh trumpet blast all of God's promises through his prophets would be fulfilled (10:5-7). The "prophets" referred to in 10:18 are Christian prophets who, like those of old, are the channels through whom God reveals his will (cf. Amos 3:7). For the imagery of the uplifted hands and the oath see Daniel 12:7; Genesis 14:22; Deuteronomy 32:40.

2. The Message to the Prophet (10:8-11). God now addresses the prophet, telling him to take the little "scroll" from the angel and "eat" it. The message of the scroll probably includes the substance of the seventh trumpet-vision and the balance of the book. Eating the scroll (10:9-10) symbolizes the thorough assimilation of God's Word into one's heart and mind, i.e., "the prophet is to become so permeated with the Word that it becomes the controlling power within" (10:9-10; cf. Jer. 15:16; 20:9; Job 23:12). The symbolism John uses here is derived from Ezekiel (2:8–3:3), although there is some variation. After Ezekiel eats his scroll he says that "it was in my mouth as sweet as honey" (3:3), but after John eats his scroll he says that "it was sweet as honey in my mouth, *but* when I had eaten it my stomach was made bitter" (10:10). The bitterness was probably caused by the woes or the wrath of God he had to proclaim in his seventh trumpet-vision and subsequently. It is indeed sweet to be admitted to the heavenly council and to be commissioned to serve as God's prophet, but a genuine prophet never "enjoys" preaching judgment and wrath.

Verse 11 reiterates the prophet's commission to prophesy (cf. 1:20); it is not a new commission, but a reaffirmation.

3. The Temple and the Two Witnesses (11:1-13). The vision of the temple and the two witnesses has been interpreted in a literal fashion by some, applying it to the persecution of the *righteous remnant in Jerusalem* by the Gentiles, the preaching of repentance by two witnesses, the virtual death of these witnesses, followed by their resurrection and ascension, and finally by the ingathering of Israel (10:1-13; 3:9; Acts 3:19 ff.; Rom. 9–11). Most interpreters, however, interpret this vision allegorically as applying to the church in the "last days." That Scripture does deal with the Jewish problem, there is no doubt (Rom. 9-11).

John, however, restricts himself to the basic clash between believers and unbelievers. We shall follow the latter interpretation below.

a. The Temple Measured (11:1-2). Here John the prophet becomes actively involved in the vision. He is commanded to measure the temple proper (*naon*), excluding the various adjacent courts, the altar, and "those who dwell there" (11:1). The symbolism of measuring in Scripture may have one of three meanings: (1) with a view to building or rebuilding (Zech. 2: 1-3; Jer. 31:39; Ezek. 40; (2) with a view to destroying (II Kings 21:13; Isa. 34:11; Amos 7:7-9); and (3) with a view to preserving or protecting in time of peril (II Sam. 8:2). It is with the last meaning in mind that the Lord tells John to measure, or seal, the temple off for protection. The temple, altar (of burnt offering), and those who worship are to be understood as referring to the faithful people of God, the new Israel (cf. I Cor. 3:16).

"The court *outside* the temple" symbolizes the world outside the church, the believing community. This space includes the Gentile Court. Jesus predicted that the "holy city" would be "trodden down by the Gentiles" (Luke 21:24; cf. Zech. 12:3). The Gentiles will subjugate and profane Jerusalem for forty-two months, or three and one-half years, but they will not utterly destroy it. The three and one-half symbolizes a time of trouble before the end, a period of limited duration (cf. Dan. 7:25; 12:7).

In 11:1-2, therefore, we see John again encourages the church in the midst of persecution, just before the last trumpet blast. God has sealed her off — she is secure in him.

b. The Two Witnesses (11:3-13). God promises to grant, give or send (*dōsō*), his "two witnesses power to prophesy" for three and one-half years, "clothed in sackcloth" (11:3). They are to prophesy, i.e., to proclaim or speak forth the inspired message of God (cf. I Cor. 14). The message they are to preach is one of repentance and coming judgment, as suggested by the "sackcloth" (cf. Jer. 4:8; 6:26; Jonah 3:5).

Who are the two witnesses? For the background for these witnesses we go to several Old Testament passages. Verse 4 immediately reminds us of Zechariah's identification of the "two olive trees," Zerubbabel the governor and Joshua the high priest, who feed their oil into a bowl which lights the lamps of a single lampstand. There "the olive trees represent the channels through which God supplies his power for work to be done."

John sees, however, two olive trees and two lampstands. The lampstands "symbolize the channels through which the might of God is to work (cf. Rev. 1:20; 2:1). Note that these two witnesses stand in close proximity to the Almighty Creator, "the Lord of the earth" (11:4). These witnesses symbolize the church militant which will prophesy for three and one half years (11:3).

Verse 5 shifts to Elijah for some imagery. Elijah called down fire from heaven against his foes (II Kings 1:10), but here John says that anyone who seeks to harm the witnesses are consumed by fire that pours forth from their mouths upon their foes (11:5; cf. II Sam. 22:9; Jer. 5:14). The witnesses who are in touch with God have phenomenal power. Like Elijah, they have power to withhold rain (11:6a; cf. I Kings 17:1; Luke 4:25; James 5:17); and like Moses, they have power to bring plagues upon the earth (11:6b; cf. Exod. 7:20).

When the time allotted to the witnesses has expired, then God permits the *Beast* (the Antichrist introduced here for the first time), who ascends from the bottomless pit, to make war against and kill the witnesses, leaving their bodies exposed "in the street of the great city" (11:7-8). The Beast was a familiar designation for the Antichrist (Dan. 7:7 ff.; Matt. 24:15). Since the witnesses represent the church, it is probably the final conflict, which is mentioned in greater detail later, that John has in mind (13:1 ff.). The "*great city* which is allegorically called Sodom and Egypt, where their Lord was crucified," is certainly Jerusalem (cf. Isa. 1:10; Deut. 32:32; Jer. 23:14; Ezek. 16:46, 49). Although the name of Egypt was not given Israel in the Old Testament, it is appropriate of her here as the enemy of God's true Israel. John mentions that the "great city" was "where their Lord was crucified," to pin point one of the sins of the hostile Jews and Gentiles.

The "dead" witnesses were left exposed in the street of Jerusalem and they were not only refused burial, but pagan peoples (Jews and Gentiles) rejoiced for three and one-half days and exchanged gifts because the witnesses who once brought conviction and a sense of guilt upon the non-Christian world were now dead (11:8-10). Again, the three and one-half days is the symbol for calamity. To leave the dead exposed was a great indignity to the Jews who usually buried their dead the day after they died (cf. Tobit 2:17 ff.). When the church *is* the church she always provokes decision, causing some to turn to Christ, and others to turn against him (cf. Acts 9:4 ff.; II Cor. 2:15-16).

But the rejoicing of the enemies of God is premature! Just when they think they have triumphed over the witnesses (the church), "a breath of life from God entered them, and they stood up on their feet, and great fear fell on those who saw them" (11:11). As Ezekiel had prophesied (37:10), so now John prophesies that God will resurrect (resuscitate) his witnesses in the sight of their enemies and call them up to heaven (11:12; cf. I Thess. 4:16-17). As a result of this miracle, those who survive the devastation of the earthquake turn and give "glory to the God of heaven" (11:13). The preceding expression is "a peculiar idiomatic phrase denoting repentance; the meaning is to pay the honor due to God by changing one's attitude and confessing, speaking, or doing, the truth as the truth of God; cf. 16:9; John 9:24; Josh. 7:19; Jer. 13:16" (Beckwith).

H. The Seventh Seal (11:14-19)

With verse 14 John resumes the presentation of the trumpet-visions which he broke off at 9:21. We would expect the last of the birth pangs of the messianic age which precede the second advent, but this evidently is still to come (chaps. 12–20). Instead, the prophet presents another proleptic picture of the kingdom of God, i.e., as having already come. In the prophet's mind there is no doubt but that the final victory is God's, therefore, he presents the picture of the consummation, and then goes on in the next several chapters to show how it will be achieved.

When the voice says that "the third woe is soon to come" (11:14), he means beginning with the seventh trumpet and subsequently.

John is now back in heaven where, after the blowing of the seventh trumpet, he hears "loud voices" saying, "the kingdom of the world *has become* the kingdom of our Lord and of his Christ, and he shall reign for ever and ever" (11:15). The rule of God "has come" and is being exercised over the kingdoms of this world — John sees this as a reality in heaven which is soon to take place on earth. Note that in the fullness of the kingdom both the Lord God and his Christ, the Anointed, shall reign for all eternity (cf. Dan. 2:44; 7:27; I Cor. 15:24-28).

The proclamation of the angelic chorus is then followed by a "hymn of thanksgiving" from the prostrated twenty-four elders. Their hymn seems to be an elaboration of verse 15. Several attributes of God are singled out for praise. First they give thanks to God for his omnipotence — "God almighty." Secondly, note they give thanks for his present reign — not for his future reign. They recognize that God's rule has always been — "who wast" — but they recognize that in a new sense it is here now (11:17).

In the last days the Gentiles will make one last assault against God's power — this they did; "but thy [God's] wrath came" and his power meant their overthrow (cf. Ps. 2:1 ff.; Rev. 16:13 ff.; 20:8 f.) Following their overthrow, the dead will be raised and judged (20:11-15). Then the "prophets and saints" and all who fear God's name, both small and great, will be rewarded (cf. 20:12 ff.; 21:1 ff.). Not only will the righteous be rewarded, but the wicked — "the destroyers" — will be destroyed (cf. 20:15; 21:8).

Finally, John is given a glimpse into the inner shrine of the temple, the holy of holies, where he sees the ark of the covenant. Jewish tradition says that the ark was carried by Jeremiah to a place of safety when the temple was destroyed, and that it would be restored to Israel when the Messiah appeared (cf. II Maccabees 2:1-8; Apocalypse of Baruch 6:7-10). At any rate, God is showing John that the fullest communion will take place in the realized kingdom because his presence will be there.

As with the seven seals (8:5) and the coming bowls (16:18), so now, the seventh plague issues in "flashes of lightning," etc., i.e., there is more to come.

VII. THE BACKGROUND OF THE CONFLICT (12:1–14:20)

We would expect that the seven bowls would follow the seventh trumpet, but instead John pauses to give extended visions which actually constitute a very crucial part of the Apocalypse. In these three chapters (12–14) he introduces us to the real nature of the struggle, which is between God and his Christ, and Satan and his diabolical forces. We shall see how the Christ has already conquered and cast Satan down. The victory is ideally won, and yet it remains to be unravelled on the stage of history. By giving the background of the struggle which is yet to unfold, the church militant can face the future with steadfast confidence.

These chapters fall neatly into another series of seven — seven scenes which move steadily on to the last series of plagues which presage the end.

A. Scene One — The Woman and Her Child (12:1-6)

Virtually all commentators call attention to the fact that this story of the woman that gives birth to a male child which is delivered from the dragon is one found in the mythology of many nations — Persian, Egyptian, Greek, etc. That John, a learned Jew of the first century, was familiar with pagan mythologies, we have little reason to doubt. Most scholars, however, emphatically emphasize that, regardless of the parallels between the visions in Revelation and other literature, John thoroughly baptized any material he drew upon into the Christian faith for his specific purpose. The Holy Spirit conveys his messages through living personalities and he uses their intellectual resources to the glory of God.

John sees a "great portent" i.e., a sign or mark (*sēmeion*) in the sense that there is a strange happening about to occur. The scene is now "in heaven," where he sees "a woman clothed with the sun, with the moon under her feet, and on her head a crown of twelve stars" (12:1). The "woman" is best understood as the "mother" of the Messiah and of Christians. She is not, however, the mother of Jesus, i.e., Mary. She is, instead, symbolic of the believing community, the righteous remnant of old Israel, from whose midst not only Christ "after the flesh" came, but also the new Israel, the Christian church (cf. Micah 4:9–5:3; Gal. 4:26). The imagery drawn upon to describe her is meant to convey her majestic dignity (cf. 1:16; Ps. 104:2; Song of Sol. 6:10; Gen. 37:9). The woman who was about to give birth, cried out for delivery (cf. 12:2; Micah 4:9 f.; Isa. 66:19).

Another sign appears introducing the enemy of the Messiah and the Christian community, the "great red dragon" (12:3). A huge serpent-like monster, quite frequently a water-monster, was a familiar object in ancient mythologies. In the Old Testament we find reference to monsters such as Leviathan, Rahab, Behemoth, a serpent, and a dragon (cf. Job. 7:12; Ps. 74:14; 89:10; Isa. 27:1; 51:9; Ezek. 32:2; Amos 9:3). This monster that embodies evil is identified with none other than Satan (12:9; cf. 20:2).

The "great red dragon" with his "seven heads" and his "ten horns, and seven diadems upon his heads" alludes to Daniel 7:1-7. In Daniel, the third beast has four heads and the fourth beast has ten horns, but here John uses these symbols, and enlarges upon them, to describe the ruler of the forces of evil, Satan (12:4, 9). Satan's goal is to destroy the Christ (the Messiah) who is to rule the nations (12:5; cf. Ps. 2:9). Well did Satan know that in the Christ his doom was sure. But when he seeks to strike against the Christ, God intervenes and the "child is caught up to God and to his throne" (12:5; cf. Phil. 2:9; Col. 2:13-15). The reference to the child caught up is to the glorious ascension of our Lord (cf. Acts 1:11).

When the "child" is taken up, then the woman, who symbolizes the church or believing community, flees into the wilderness to a place prepared by God, where she is to be nourished for a limited time — three and one-half years (12:6). The church is safe during the period of Antichrist's persecution (cf. 7:1-8; 9:1-2). We shall return to Satan's persecution of the church later (12:13-17).

B. Scene Two — The War in Heaven (12:7-12)

Upon first reading 12:7-12 it might appear that the archangel Michael and his angels are responsible for the overthrow of Satan, but verse 11 makes it clear that the Dragon was conquered "by the blood of the Lamb and by the word of their testimony." It was only because Jesus Christ had poured out his life blood that Satan could be overcome (cf. Heb. 2:14-15), and we overcome the forces of evil in the same way, by identification with Christ (cf. Phil. 3:10-11; Gal. 2:20).

Satan was thought to dwell in the lower sphere of heaven (cf. Eph. 2:2; Luke 10:18). He had access to God's presence and is described as the chief foe of the saints, i.e., "the accuser of the brethren (cf. Job 1:6 ff.; Zech. 3:1 ff.). The Hebrew and Greek meaning of the name "devil" means "slanderer." John tells us clearly that the goal of Satan, now that he and his angels have been cast out of heaven, is to deceive and attack the saints (12:9, 13 ff.).

Note that when Satan is cast out, the kingdom of God comes in a new way: "And I heard a loud voice in heaven, saying, 'Now the salvation and the power and the kingdom of our God and the authority of his Christ *have come,* for the accuser of our brethren *has been* thrown down, who accuses them day and night before our God" (12:10). We are reminded of the crucial passage in John's Gospel (12:20-36a) where Satan's overthrow by the cross-resurrection is predicted. Satan, who was being overthrown by the exorcisms of our Lord and his disciples, was decisively defeated by the triumph of Christ, as John pictures so graphically here (12:7-10). But not only did Christ defeat Satan; the saints then, and now, also defeat him "by the word of their testimony" and their total commitment to Christ (12:11). Satan is powerless against the believer who is "in Christ." While the heavens and those within it are called to rejoice because Satan has been cast down, those upon the earth and the sea are called to be on guard, for Satan is now directing his wiles against them for a limited time (12:12-14).

C. Scene Three — The Persecution of the Woman (the Church) (12:13-17)

The "woman" in 12:13 symbolizes the church, the believing community of old Israel and of the new Israel. It was out of a "righteous remnant" the Messiah was born, and now this "righteous remnant" continues their faithful witness to their Lord. The church was given eagle wings that she might flee from the "serpent" (Satan) into the wilderness to the place which God had prepared for her (12:6, 14; cf. Isa. 40:31). The persecution was to last a limited time (12:6, 14). When the "church" fled, the serpent, who had become a "sea monster," pursued her to the shore. From his mouth the serpent poured forth a river of water in an effort to destroy the "church," but God caused the earth to come to the aid of the believing community by opening its mouth and swallowing the water (12:15-16; cf. Isa. 43:2a). Frustrated with his attempt to destroy this part of the "church," he turns "to make war on the rest of her off-spring" or seed — these, like those in the wilderness, were "those who keep (hold fast) the commandments of God and bear testimony to Jesus (12:17).

Many see an analogy between the last scene (12:13-17) and the Exodus and wilderness experience of Israel. Undoubtedly John had something like it in mind. What he is affirming here is God's providential deliverance and care for his people. When the waters of life threaten the "church," God has, and will, deliver his own (cf. Isa. 43:2; I Cor. 10:13). But the serpent (Satan) never rests — he continually goes about seeking to devour the believing community (cf. I Peter 5:8).

D. Scene Four — The Sea Beast (12:17b—13:10)

The serpent now seeks to deceive men by two avenues: (1) ruthless totalitarian government (13:1-10), and (2) its ally, false religion (13:11-18).

At the close of the last scene the serpent-sea monster was standing "on the sand of the sea" (12:17b). The present scene opens with "a beast rising out of the sea." This Sea Beast has "ten horns and seven heads, with ten diadems upon its heads, with a blasphemous name upon its heads" (13:1). For the background for this chapter see Daniel 7:1 ff. The sea usually refers to corrupt human government and the Sea Beast represents the diabolical emperors of Rome who embody all the vile qualities of the four beasts of Daniel 7. The "ten horns" refer to the allied kings of Rome, each of whom is crowned with a diadem (or crown.) — a mark of kingly rank. The "seven heads" refer to the successive emperors of Rome (cf. 17:5 ff.). "Blasphemous" names or titles were ascribed to the emperors, Domitian and Caligula being especially noted for their "god intoxication." By the end of the first century A.D., the emperors were worshiped as the incarnation of deity.

In describing the Sea Beast John draws upon Daniel 7:2 ff. (13:2). The "leopard" suggests the Beast's "cruelty and cunning," the "feet . . . like bear's" suggests his strength, and his "mouth . . . like a lion" suggests his ferocity. John makes it clear that the source of the diabolical rulers of Rome eminated from the Dragon (Devil) himself (13:2b).

The interpretations of verse 3 are legion, but the concensus seems to be that the head with the "mortal wound" which was healed refers to the common belief that Nero, who committed suicide in A.D. 68, was to return again from the dead to make war on the saints (cf. 5:6). This figure represents the Antichrist figure who is to appear at the end of the age (cf. 19:19). So amazing is the Beast's return that all of those who are not committed to Christ follow him (13:3; cf. I Tim. 5:15).

The world apart from Christ worshiped the "Dragon" and his

agent, the Beast, to whom he had given power and authority (13:2, 4). Then, as now, the powers of evil seem irresistable — "Who is like the beast, and who can fight against it?" (13:4a).

In the next paragraph the blasphemous nature of the Sea Beast is described. The "haughty and blasphemous words" which he utters are probably claims of deity that the emperors made for themselves (13:5-6). Domitian insisted that his subjects address him as "Lord and God." We are reminded of the passage in Daniel where similar blasphemies were uttered (Dan. 7:8, 20, 25; 8:12, 24; 11:28, 30, 32).

It is of great importance to note John's faith in the sovereignty of God. The Antichrist who exercises power for a limited time, three and a half years, operates within the permissive will of God — this is clearly seen in verse 7 where we read, "Also it [the Sea Beast] was *allowed* to make war on the saints." The Beast's power over the nations was "given" to him and all those whose names were not "written before the foundation of the world in the book of life of the Lamb that was slain," worshiped him (13:7-8; cf. 3:5; 17:8).

Verses 9 and 10 constitute a call to the saints for steadfastness and faithfulness (cf. Jer. 15:2 for a similar thought). Verse 10 is not advocating pacificism, but advising believers to accept without resistance whatever the providence of God sends — even martyrdom.

E. Scene Five — The Land Beast (13:11-18)

In the second part of this vision John sees a second beast arising from the land (13:11). This Land Beast personifies the priesthood of the pagan Emperor Cult which helps entice men to worship the first Beast — who represents the emperor and the Antichrist (13:12). The Land Beast, by contrast, is not as ferocious or as powerful as the first — he has only two horns. Although he simulates the Lamb, his words are devilish (Beasley-Murray). He makes no claims of deity, but he uses his speech to deceive men (13:11b, 14). Later we shall see that the Land Beast and the False Prophet are one and the same person (cf. 15:13; 19:20; 20:10).

John describes the diabolical trickery which the pagan priestly cultus worked (13:13-15). They worked all sorts of "miracles" to convince their superstitious public of the power of their deity — ventriloquism was a common device (13:15). Many Jews and early Christians believed that miracles would precede the coming of the Antichrist (cf. Mark 13:22 f.; II Thess. 2:9-10).

Those who refused to worship the image of the Beast were to be slain (13:15).

The control of the corrupt totalitarian state reached through its religion to control the lives of its people. If men wished to participate in the daily civic and social life, i.e., buy and sell, they were compelled to bear the name, i.e., number of the Sea Beast (Emperor) upon their right hand or forehead (13:16-17). Beckwith states that the practice of having the name or sign of the deity upon one's body was quite common in the ancient world. Ptolemy Philadelphus compelled certain Alexandrian Jews to receive the mark of Dionysus (III Maccabees 2:29; cf. Isa. 44:5; Gal. 6:17). The Jews of the first century often wore phylacteries upon their left hand or their brow.

Just whom the "human number" of 666 (or 616 as some manuscripts have it) represents is difficult to say. By computing the numerical values of the letters of the "Beast's" name, his identity is often made. Many ingenious attempts have been made to identify this person. The most frequent historical identification has been that of the *emperor Nero* who was believed to be dead but soon to return to life. "If the name of the emperor is expressed in the Greek form, 'Neron Caesar,' and then rewritten in Hebrew letters, with the values which they have in the Hebrew alphabet, the result is exactly 666. It is perhaps significant that if we take the more familiar Latin form, 'Nero Caesar,' the result is 616, and this number actually occurs at this point in some of the Greek manuscripts of our New Testament" (Love). But although the concensus of scholarly opinion identifies 666 or 616 with Nero Caesar, the prophet John doubtlessly has a more significant person in mind — the Antichrist. All antichrists which appear on the scene of history, whether they be Nero Caesar or any of the numerous diabolical totalitarians down to our day, are only 666 — woefully lacking.

John says: "This calls for wisdom: let him who has understanding reckon the number of the beast, for it is a human number . . ." (13:18).

F. Scene Six — The Lamb and the Redeemed Host (14:1-5)

From the awful threatening picture of the church being persecuted by the *two agents* of the Dragon, John reveals two visions: *one* which portrays the glory which awaits the suffering saints at the second coming of Christ (14:1-5; cf. 21:9 ff.; Joel 2:32), and *another* which reveals the judgment which is in store for the wicked (14:6-20).

John sees the Lamb standing on Mount Zion with 144,000

who have the name of the Lamb and God upon their fore-heads (14:1). There is an obvious connection between this scene and that of the "Lamb standing, as though it had been slain," and the 144,000 referred to in an earlier scene (cf. 5:6 ff.; 7:4 ff.). The 144,000 symbolize all the redeemed of God — those who have been faithful to the Christ through their trials and testings.

There is some question whether this Mount Zion is on earth or in heaven. It seems, however, that the scene is a preview of the New Jerusalem which will be revealed in the Millennial Age.

Verses 2 and 3 seem to indicate that the singers about the throne are not the 144,000, but some angelic chorus. These sing-ers teach the song of praise and redemption to the 144,000. Only the faithful witnesses are privileged to learn and sing this new song (14:3b). John refers to the redeemed host which is taught the "new song" as those "who have not defiled themselves with women, for they are chaste" (Gk. virgins) (14:4a). This does not refer to celibates as some maintain, but to moral purity and fidelity to Christ (cf. II Cor. 11:2). In prophetic literature, apos-tacy and rebellion are often expressed by the figure of "adultery" or "unfaithfulness" (cf. Jer. 5:7; Hos. 2:1 ff.). Those who follow the Lamb in the New Age are those "who have been redeemed from mankind as first fruits for God and the Lamb" (14:4b). The word "first fruits" (*aparchē*) really refers to the sacrifice of the first fruits. The sacrifice of the first fruits was the best of the crop and John uses this to symbolize the holiness and dedi-cation which characterizes the redeemed (cf. Deut. 26:1-11; Lev. 23:10-14; Rom. 16:15; I Cor. 15:20). The church, the bride of Christ, is seen as sinless and spotless by virtue of the finished work of Christ — the redeemed become like the Redeemer (14:5; cf. Zeph. 3:13; Phil. 3:21; I John 3:1-3).

G. The Interlude — the Day of Wrath and Blessing (14:6-13)

1. The Call to Repentance (14:6-7). John now turns to call men to repentance in the face of God's impending day of wrath (14:6-12). Three angels are introduced, each with a specific message for unrepentant sinners, followers of the Beast.

The first angel proclaims the "eternal gospel" or the "Good News" to all the inhabitants of the earth. The gospel is that mys-tery which heretofore has been hidden, but now has been re-vealed by *the work, and through the person of Jesus Christ* (14:6; cf. Eph. 3:8-13). Jesus said that before the *end* the gospel would be preached to all nations (Mark 13:10). The angel calls men to turn from idolatrous pagan worship and "give God the glory" because "the *hour* of his judgment has come" (14:7a). In his Gospel John records the words of Jesus who said that *after* the "hour" in which man is privileged to respond to the Good News is past, man will experience the "hour" of judgment (John 5:25-29). Here he reiterates that truth. It is none other than the Creator God whom the angels call men to worship.

2. The Day of Wrath (14:8-11). The second angel announces the fall of "Babylon the great." She has fallen because she has seduced other nations to follow her in licentious idolatry and all manner of evil. Babylon here is a symbol of Rome, but she also symbolizes every totalitarian power that seduces men, and also "the Babylon" at the end of history (cf. Dan. 4:30-31; Jer. 51: 7-8; I Peter 5:13). The fall of Babylon (Rome) is treated in full detail in Chapter 18.

Not only does the angel announce the doom of the "Babylonian state" but also the wrath of God against all those who worship the Beast and receive his mark (14:9-10). The angel says that those who refuse to repent "shall drink the wine of God's wrath, poured unmixed into the cup of his anger." The figure of the cup of God's wrath is frequently used to convey God's terrible judgment (cf. Jer. 25:15; Job 21:20; Ps. 75:8; Isa. 51:17). "Unmixed" wine suggests the undiluted wrath of God.

The punishment of the wicked is made most unbearable because it will be experienced in the presence of "the holy angels" and "the Lamb" (14:10; cf. Luke 16:23).

Verse 11 makes it clear that there is no second chance after death — those who worship the Beast suffer *for ever and ever.*

3. The Word to the Believers (14:12-13). John pauses to appeal to the *saints* on earth to "hold fast," i.e., all those who are "keeping the commandments of God" and (have) "faith *in* Jesus," not keep the faith *of* Jesus. The Revised Standard Version translators overlooked the objective genitive.

In contrast to the word of judgment for the wicked, our Lord gives John a message to encourage the saints. Those who die "*in* the Lord" are indeed blessed (cf. I Thess. 4:16), for they are assured of resurrection on that great day. Not only are they "blessed indeed" because they "rest from their labors," but because "their deeds follow them" (14:13). Their deeds follow them in two ways: (1) their witness leaves a salutary example for the saints on earth, and (2) their deeds will be a witness to their faithfulness to Christ at the last judgment (I Cor. 15: 58; 3:14; Rev. 20:13).

H. Scene Seven — the Judgment of the World (14:14-20)

In this last scene John presents a picture of world judgment, which he develops later in 19:11-21. The "one like a son of man" seated on the cloud is either Christ or an angelic servant. Some scholars feel that it could not be Christ because he is commanded by an angel to reap the harvest (14:15). There seems to be no reason, however, to deny that the "Son of Man" in verse 14 is the Christ. "The *hour* to reap has come," i.e., the hour appointed by God for judgment. The Lord is pictured as having returned to execute the judgment of God, even as he will return to reward the saints (cf. 14:15-16; Matt. 13:36-43; 25:31 ff.; II Thess. 1:7 ff.).

Another angel, a sixth, comes forth "from the altar" to aid the Son of Man in the harvest (14:18; cf. 6:9-11; 8:1-5; 9:13; 16:7). He is directed by a seventh angel who had power over fire, perhaps Gabriel, whom Jewish tradition assigned this task. The symbol used in 14:18-20 to convey the wrath of God is the familiar figure of the treading of the wine press of God's wrath found in Isaiah 63:3 and Joel 3:13.

Note that "the wine press was trodden outside the city," probably outside Jerusalem where our Lord was crucified (cf. Heb. 13:12). John says that the blood flowed for 1600 stadia, about 200 miles, perhaps suggesting the length of Palestine.

This last scene sets the stage for the introduction of the last series of seven woes, the seven bowls.

VIII. THE VISION OF THE SEVEN BOWLS (15:1–16:21)

In this last series of woes, the seven bowls, a fuller revelation of the judgment of God is given, which builds upon the one given in the seals and the trumpets. As a result of these plagues, the "great-harlot" city, "Babylon," falls, and with her topples all the forces of evil.

A. Preparation for the Seven Bowls (15:1-8)

John picks up in 15:1 where the seventh trumpet ended (11: 15-19). The first verse serves as an introduction for the next two chapters. The vision is "great and wonderful" because it presents encouragement to the suffering saints by announcing the certain overthrow of the forces of evil. These seven angels which he sees will soon pour out the *final* plagues — "seven golden bowls full of the wrath of God who lives for ever and ever" (15:1, 7). After the forces of evil are overthrown, comes the final judgment, followed by the Millennial Age.

The preparatory vision is divided into two parts: 15:2-4 pictures the victorious Christians who sing a song of praise to God, and 15:5-8 is a vision of the seven angels with the seven bowls.

1. The Song of Moses and of the Lamb (15:2-4). Verse 2 gives John and the saints an anticipatory picture of the glory which awaits those who "come off victorious from the" (Gk.) Beast by refusing to worship his image, or to be stamped with the number of his name (666). The saints stand by the glassy sea (of the Throne room 4:6 ?) which is mingled with fire. Perhaps the fire suggests the fire of judgment which is soon to descend upon the world. Some see here a reference to the Red Sea (Exod. 15:1 ff.) because of the mention of the "song of Moses" in 15:3. The "harps of God" which they hold belong to the heavenly worship (cf. 5:8; 14:2; I Chron. 16:42).

The song of Moses and of the Lamb which they sing link the two great redemptive acts of the Hebrew-Christian Religion. Moses had led the *old Israel* from bondage to the Egyptians, and the Lamb who had been slain delivered all mankind from spiritual bondage. Those who accept the grace of God in Christ constitute the "new Israel" of God.

The actual song they sing is composed of utterances from the Old Testament. Note that the song lauds the God who has acted in history ("deeds," "ways") and acclaims him as sovereign Lord of history ("Almighty," "King of the ages or nations") (15:3; cf. Ps. 111:2; 139:14; Amos 4:13; Deut. 32:4; Ps. 145:17; Jer. 10:7).

The last stanza reiterates the prophecy of the Old Testament prophets that "all nations shall come and worship Thee" (God), i.e., in *the end* all shall acknowledge Jehovah as sovereign "because of the manifestations of God's righteous acts of judgment" (15:4; cf. Phil. 2:11; I Cor. 15:24 ff.; Isa. 2:2-4; 66:23).

2. The Giving of the Seven Bowls (15:5-8). John now proceeds to describe what he saw when "the temple of the tent of witness in heaven was opened" (15:5). The temple was sometimes called "the tent, or tabernacle of testimony" (Exod. 38:21; Num. 9:15; 10:11; Acts 7:44) "because it contained the ark, or the tables, of the testimony, the ten commandments, which declared the nature and will of God" (Beckwith). The fact that the seven angels came out of the temple suggest that the judgments they are to deliver are expressions of God's righteous and holy will. "Their pure linen and their golden girdles at their breasts (vs. 6) are emblematic of their priestly function in worship; yet they are the bearers of the full measure of God's wrath on the unrepentant earth" (Love.).

God sent to these seven angels, one of the four living creatures "with seven bowls full of the wrath of God who lives for ever and ever" (15:7; cf. 4:6). The bowls (*phialas*) were shallow bowl-shaped vessels that were used especially for drinking and libations. "In 14:8, 10 the wrath of God is a deadly wine which is given men to drink, a cup . . . which sinners must drain; here the metaphor is changed, the cup becomes an open bowl, pouring out its burning contents upon the earth . . ." (Swete).

The manifestation of God's glory and power are symbolized by the smoke which filled the temple, a familiar symbol in the Old Testament (Exod. 24:16, 40:34-38; I Kings 8:10 f.; etc.). John adds that "no one could enter the temple until the seven plagues of the seven angels were ended," i.e., to intercede with God for him to revoke his judgment. This smoke continued until the voice in the temple cried, "It is done!" (16:17).

B. The Seven Bowls (16:1-21)

Once the seven angels are given the seven bowls they go forth in obedience to the voice from the temple which commands them to "go and pour out on the earth the seven bowls of the wrath of God" (16:1; cf. 11:14). These plagues are reminiscent of those worked by God through Moses in Egypt and most of them resemble the trumpet plagues, only the devastation they work is complete.

1. The First Bowl (16:2). The plague of "foul and evil sores" which follows the outpouring of the first bowl effects all the inhabitants of the earth, whereas the first trumpet plague only covered one third of the inhabitants (cf. 8:7). The *sores* are reminiscent of the plague upon the Egyptians and symbolize some punishment which will fall upon the followers of the Beast (cf. Exod. 9:10-11; Deut. 28:35).

2. The Second Bowl (16:3). This plague is likewise more extensive than the second trumpet plague. The entire sea is here polluted by a coagulating and decaying, bloody substance which causes all life in the sea to die (cf. Exod. 7:17-21; Rev. 8:8-9).

3. The Third Bowl (16:4-7). This third bowl is poured into the sources of man's drinking water and causes it to be turned into blood (Exod. 7:20). The third trumpet plague turned one-third of rivers and fountains to wormwood (8:9-11). The "angel of water" sings a song in praise of God's holiness and justice which is reminiscent of the song in 15:3-4. But the angel introduces a new note of retribution — God will cause those who have martyred the saints (Christians in general), and prophets (a class of preachers within the church) to perish by the sword. This seems to be the meaning of "thou hast given them blood to drink" (16:6; cf. Isa. 49:26). This judgment, says the angel, "is their due."

To this announcement of God's judgment the "altar," which is a personification of the saints who abide under the altar, utters words of approval (16:7; cf. 6:10; 14:18; 19:1-2).

4. The Fourth Bowl (16:8-9). The fourth bowl is poured upon the sun, thereby including four spheres of nature in God's judgment — earth, sea, rivers and fountains, and sun.

The heat of the sun is not diminished by this plague, but rather it is intensified so that men are scorched. Men see the hand of God's judgment in this plague, but instead of repenting and giving glory to God in repentance and faith, they curse the name of God. We are reminded of Paul's summary of man's rebellion against God in Romans (1:18-23; cf. Amos 4:6-12).

5. The Fifth Bowl (16:10-11). The contents of the fifth bowl is poured upon the "throne of the Beast" and it causes darkness to spread through the Beast's kingdom (16:10a; cf. Exod. 10:21

ff.; Rev. 2:13). Some think the "pain and sores" which afflict the disciples of the Beast are caused by the locusts of the fifth trumpet plague (9:1-6). This might well be the case, for the reference to "plagues" in 16:9 and the "pains and sores" in 16:11 (cf. 16:2) seem to suggest that several plagues were co-existent. Just as the judgment of the fourth bowl did not produce repentance, neither did the judgment of the fifth bowl; instead, the wicked continue in their impenitence and refuse to turn to God (16:11).

6. The Sixth Bowl (16:12-16). The contents of the sixth bowl is poured out upon "the great river Euphrates," resulting in the drying up of the waters, thus making it possible for "the kings from the east" to come against the saints at *Armageddon* (16:12, 16). Many see here the Roman fear that the Parthians, led by Nero, whom many believed would be restored to life, might attack Rome. God will use the ruthless Parthians to destroy evil Rome, but there is certainly more to be found here in this sixth bowl than a contemporary reference to Rome and the Parthians. This was probably the "short range" reference, but the "long range" application is to the final conflict which will precede the coming of the millennium. This reference to the final conflict is made clear in verses 13-16. John sees issuing from the mouth of the "trinity of evil" — the Dragon (Satan), the (Sea) Beast (false totalitarian government), and the False Prophet (he is identical to the Land Beast who symbolizes false religion) — "three foul spirits like frogs." We are told what these spirits symbolize, namely, "demonic spirits" which work signs or miracles that are instrumental in bringing "the kings of the whole world" together for the final conflict, the "battle on the great day of God the Almighty" (16:13-14). The kings of the whole world (16:13-14) are identical with those in 17:12-14.

The name for God used here is *El Shaddai,* the name which connotes power, the name the covenant making God gave to Abraham (Gen. 17:1).

Verse 15 is a parenthetical ejaculatory word of warning and encouragement which was to stimulate the believers to hold fast. This verse is an elaboration of 3:3, and reflects the words of our Lord (Matt. 24:43), of Paul (I Thess. 5:2, 4), and of Peter (II Peter 3:10).

The kings of the whole earth assemble at a "place which is called in Hebrew *Armageddon*" (16:16). Armageddon or *Har-Magedon* literally means "mount of plagues" or "mount of Megiddo." It is commonly understood that the reference is to the Plain of Esdraelon, at one end of which was located Megiddo

(G. A. Smith). The region of Megiddo was the classic battle-ground of Old Testament Scripture — the scene of many crucial battles (Judges 5; II Kings 6:17, 23; Zech. 12:11). John is probably using the name *Armageddon* in some mystical, symbolic sense. It is the place where Satan shall gather the forces of Antichrist on that Great Day (cf. 19:11 ff.).

7. The Seventh Bowl (16:17-21). When the seventh bowl is poured out into the air, the greatest and most devastating results follow (16:17).

The fact that the bowl is poured into the air suggests that that which is vital to all life is effected. It is God's final attack upon the diabolical forces which oppose him, both human and spiritual (cf. Eph. 2:2). When the bowl was poured out, a voice cries out from the temple proclaiming the end of the diabolical kingdom of evil — "It is done." Earlier our Lord Jesus said from the cross, "It is finished. (John 19:30). Christ had paid the price of redemption which made the final triumph over evil certain, and now John proclaims proleptically the complete victory over evil.

The cataclysmic signs which mark the end are "flashes of lightning, loud noises, peals of thunder, and a great earthquake . . ." (16:18). This plague results not in the destruction of Babylon, the city of the Antichrist, but in its break up into three parts. The allied nations of the Beast, however, are overthrown. Babylon, who caused the other nations to drink "the wine of her impure passion" is now made to "drain the cup of the fury of his [God's] wrath" (16:19; cf. 14:8; 18:3).

Verse 20 refers not to the dissolution of the earth, but to the sinking of islands and mountains because of the earthquake. In Jewish literature this is a familiar sign associated with the end (cf. Assumption of Moses 10:4; I Enoch 1:6). The tremendous hail stones are also a sign of the end. Instead of God's judgment producing repentance, men turn from God and curse him. Cf. Exodus 9:24; Joshua 10:11; Isaiah 28:2 and Ezekiel 38:22 where similar phenomena are recorded.

IX. THE JUDGMENT OF BABYLON — THE GREAT HARLOT (17:1-18)

In these next three chapters John presents a series of visions which culminate in the destruction of the Beast and the False Prophet. In the sixth and seventh bowl John foretold the final conflict which was to take place at "Armageddon" which would result in final victory — "It is done" (16:12-21). Now in Chapter 17 he prophesies of the fall of Babylon, which symbolizes not only Rome but the kingdom of Antichrist, and then in Chapter 18 many angels utter a dirge against Babylon.

A. The Harlot and the Beast (17:1-6a)

John is invited to view the judgment which is to come upon the Harlot, the great city, Babylon (17:1, 16, 18). The "great harlot" is identified by the angel with Babylon and the empire of the Antichrist. The allusion to her being seated upon many waters may be to Jeremiah 51:13. The river Euphrates actually passed through the ancient city of Babylon. In 17:15 we are told that the waters represent the peoples and nations over whom "Babylon" has dominion. Those who have consorted with the "great harlot" have corrupted themselves (17:2).

The angel, one who had one of the seven bowls, carried John in the Spirit into the wilderness where he saw a woman, the great harlot, seated on a "scarlet beast" (17:3). The wilderness means a deserted area which may have been near a sea (Isa. 21:1). The "scarlet beast" which "was full of blasphemous names and had seven heads and ten horns" probably refers to the diabolical empire of the Antichrist and its leader, the Beast (17:3; cf. 17:8 ff.).

The attire of the Harlot symbolizes the affluence of Babylon (17:4). Barclay sas she is pictured as a "wealthy courtesan" standing ready to seduce men (nations). She is pictured as holding a "golden cup" which contains, not wine for her votaries, but evil enticements to lure men into her corrupt train. Her forehead reveals the name which symbolizes her true nature. Moffatt suggests that "a name of mystery" (*mustērion*) should be translated "a name by way of symbol." The title on her forehead was in keeping with the custom of that day which called for the display of the harlot's name on her brow (17:5).

Verse 6 probably refers to the custom of taking martyrs to Rome for execution. The "saints" may be a general reference which John makes specific by identifying the saints as those who shed their life blood as "witnesses" (*marturōn*) of Jesus (cf. 16:6).

B. The Angel Interprets the Vision (17:6b-18)

John, puzzled by the vision of the Harlot and the Beast, has it interpreted to him by an angel (17:7). The explanation extends through 19:21. "The beast that was, and is not, and is to ascend from the bottomless pit and go to perdition" will be marveled at by all those whose names were not written in the "book of life from the foundation of the world" (17:8; cf. 13:8). The thing that causes them to marvel is that the "beast" who once "died" is believed to have returned to life (17:8; cf. 11:7). Most interpreters identify the "beast" with the prevalent belief of *Nero Revivivus,* but in its ultimate sense he symbolizes the Antichrist of the last day.

In 17:9-10 the seven heads are identified with the seven hills on which the capital city of the diabolical empire of Rome stood. But they not only symbolize the seven hills of Rome but they *also* symbolize the seven kings or emperors of the Roman Empire. Of these seven kings, five have already died, one is now ruling, and soon a seventh will reign for "a little while." After this seventh king, the one "that was and is not" *will* come again. To him will be gathered "ten kings" who are symbolized by "ten horns" (17:11-12; cf. 17:3, 7). It should be noted that these "ten kings" have *not yet* received royal power, but they will receive it from the eighth king. The extent of their power will be only for a brief time — "one hour" — because the time is short and the end is at hand (17:12). Just exactly who these ten kings are is not certain. The historical setting of the first century might have suggested the satraps who ruled the Parthians with whom *Nero Redivius* was to come (17:12-13; cf. 16:12). But since ten is a round number, they are best taken to be the allies of the Antichrist in the last days. These will make war against the Lamb and the saints (the "chosen and faithful"), but the Lamb will conquer them for he is "Lord of lords and King of kings."

John gives us in verse 14 a summary statement of the victory that will be elaborated in 19:11-21 where the prophecy that the beast shall go "to perdition," (17:11) is fulfilled (19:20).

As stated earlier, "the waters" symbolize the allies of the Beast (17:15; cf. Isa. 8:7; Jer. 47:2). The Beast and his allied kings ironically turn upon the Harlot, the diabolical Empire, and destroy her as God had predetermined. The figure employed by John to symbolize the destruction of the Harlot is a familiar one in prophetic literature (17:16; cf. Micah 3:3; Zeph. 3:3; Jer. 10:25).

Verse 18 makes it clear beyond doubt whom the woman, the Harlot, represented, namely, "Babylon" who has dominion over the kings of the earth.

This seventeenth chapter is both an elaboration of the sixth and seventh bowl and the visions of Chapter thirteen. John gives a glimpse of the great battle of Armageddon which is about to take place, and he assures the "chosen and faithful" saints that the victory belongs to the Lamb who had already conquered by his death (cf. 1:5-6; 5:5 ff.; etc.).

X. LAMENTATIONS AND THANKSGIVING OVER THE FALL OF BABYLON (18:1–19:10)

In Chapter eighteen John records the judgment of God against Babylon. The style of the poem is similar to the dirges in the Old Testament against Babylon (Isa. 21:47) and Tyre (Ezek. 26–27).

It is interesting to observe how closely the false religion of Babylon is intertwined with greed and avarice on the part of nations and merchants. "The love of money," i.e., for material things, is the *root* of all evil, whether it is the goal of Babylon of old, or some modern "Babylon" who has rebelled against God. The consequences are the same — inevitable destruction.

A. The Certain Downfall of Babylon (18:1-3)

An angel with great authority, i.e., power to speak so that all might hear, came down from heaven to announce the downfall of Babylon. Note the use of the "past tense" which is really prophetic and expresses the certainty of the future event. When the angel appears the earth is "made bright with his splendor" — this reminds us of the *shekinah glory* of God which returns to the temple of Jerusalem after it is rebuilt (18:1-2; cf. Ezek. 43:2).

Babylon (Rome) has fallen (17:2; cf. Isa. 21:9). It has become "a haunt of every foul spirit" etc., i.e., it is a place where "demons and birds of prey watch for their prey" (17:2; cf. Isa. 13:21-22; I Peter 3:19). The reason given for her destruction is the corrupting influence she has had upon kings and merchants. She has led them astray by causing them to drink "the wine of her impure passion." Part of the way in which the nations have been corrupted was through unscrupulous merchants who used Babylon's craving for luxuriousness or wantonness to their own advantage.

B. God's People Are Warned to Flee from Babylon (18:4-5)

God (or Christ) calls now for the saints to flee from the wicked city whose doom is certain (18:4; cf. Jer. 51:45; 51:6; 50:8; Isa. 48:20; 53:11). We are reminded of Paul's admonition to the Corinthian Christians to separate themselves from the world which is hostile to God and his children (II Cor. 6:17; cf. I John 2:15-17; James 4:4).

The thought conveyed by the statement "her sins are heaped high as heaven" is that the sins *"cleave to one another,* forming a mass reaching unto heaven" — so multitudinous are Babylon's sins (18:5; cf. Jer. 51:9; Ezra 9:6). Although it looks as though the wicked go unpunished, John reminds his readers that "God remembers" and in his own time he will come with judgment.

C. A Cry for Vengeance to Be Executed against Babylon (18:6-8)

The Lord calls for those who are to execute vengeance to come and punish Babylon. Babylon has been ruthless and oppressive, and now God will meet out to her double for all her wickedness (18:6-7a; cf. Isa. 40:2; Jer. 50:15, 29). She will be compelled to drink from the very cup she prepared for others (18:6-7a; cf. 16:8; 17:4). Just as Babylon once bathed in luxury, so she shall taste the depth of degradation (18:17a; cf. Isa. 3:16-26).

The boasting of Rome reminds us of the arrogant pride of Tyre and Babylon in the Old Testament. In Isaiah (47:8b) Babylon said: "I am, and there is no one besides me; I shall not sit as a widow or know loss of children," but the Lord prophesied doom upon her and it came to pass. Here God promises again that "Babylon," because of her arrogant pride, shall be destroyed suddenly, "in a single day," by the invading hosts led by the Antichrist (18:8; cf. 17:16; Jer. 50:34).

D. A Lamentation over Babylon (18:9-19)

In this section those who partook of Babylon's sins lament her passing. The background here seems to be Ezekiel's description of the judgment of the city of Tyre (Ezek. 26—28).

1. The Kings of the Earth (18:9-10). The nations who lament the destruction of "the mighty city, Babylon" are those over whom she has dominion (18:9; cf. 17:18; Ezek. 26:16 f.; 27:35). John's favorite figure for the destruction of Babylon is fire (18:9; cf. 18:8, 17; 19:3; Isa. 34:10; Ezek. 28:18). The kings, merchants, and shipmasters all witness the swift destruction of the harlot city — "in one hour" (18:10, 17, 19).

2. The Merchants of the Earth (18:11-17a). When Babylon falls, so does her empire, bringing industry and trade to a virtual standstill. Therefore, the merchants of the earth weep and lament because there is no one to buy her wares (18:11). Compare Ezekiel 27:12-24 for a similar list of commodities that the nations traded with Tyre (18:12-13). The "thyine wood," or "scented wood," may refer specifically to thyme wood which grew in North Africa, or to a variety of scented woods (citron,

cedar, or sandal) that was used to make costly furniture. *"Ivory"* was popular among the Romans. Then, even as today in Asia and the Near East, it is used for decorating furniture. *"Anamon"* (*amōmon*) is "a perfume or ointment made from an oriental plant of the name, whose identification is uncertain" (Beckwith). The *"spice"* is an unguent often used on the hair. The *"chariots"* is the only reference that does not have a parallel in Ezekiel's list. It is a rare word believed to be of Gallic origin, referring to a carriage with four wheels, often excessively ornamented. Turner thinks the word translated chariot (*rhedōn*) is a misunderstanding of the Hebrew word *redhidhi* meaning "women's finery."

The list concludes with a reference to the slave traffic. The Revised Standard Version is correct in translating the last phrase, "slaves, that is, human souls" (18:13). There is no reference here to two classes of slaves as some suppose. "Perhaps John employed both terms to express his abhorance at so brutal a system that crushed men's bodies and souls alike" (Beasley-Murray) (cf. Ezek. 27:13).

Verse 14 is addressed directly to Babylon by the prophet John. The once affluent city is now utterly stripped of her material splendor. Just as the kings stood at a distance and lamented the fall of Babylon, so do the merchants grieve the fact that the Harlot City no longer is decked out with all the finery she once knew (18:15-16; cf. 17:4).

3. The Shipmasters and Sailors (18:17b-19). On that Great Day all those who do business at sea – "Those who go down to the sea in ships" – will join the kings and merchants in their lamentation. They shall stand aghast and cry, "What city was like the great city?" (18:18; cf. Ezek. 27:32). Quite naturally the shipmasters cast ashes upon their heads, for their source of wealth has gone up in smoke – "in one [short] hour she has been laid waste" (18:19; cf. Ezek. 27:30).

4. A Call for Rejoicing (18:20). The prayer of the martyred saints beneath the altar (6:9) and others for vindication is here answered. The Prophet, John, cries out to the heavens, and to the saints in general, and to the apostles and prophets in particular, to rejoice because God has heard their cry and answered with judgment. Babylon has fallen, as the angel in 18:21 ff. declared (cf. 12:12; Jer. 51:48; Isa. 44:23). In 19:1-7 the multitude in heaven joins in a mighty Hallelujah Chorus in gratitude for the victory over Babylon.

E. The Fall of Babylon Symbolized (18:21-24)

John sees a vision in which "a mighty angel" casts a millstone into the sea. The angel then interprets his actions to John. This vision of the millstone illustrates how Babylon shall be destroyed, never to rise again (18:21; cf. Jer. 51:63-64). Whereas 18:9-19 described the ruin of Babylon in relation to the world outside, here in verses 22-23a, the angel tells of the terrible effect within the actual city. All semblance of pleasure (music), business and industry (craftsman and millstone), or family life (voice of the bridegroom) are gone (cf. Jer. 25:10; 7:34; Isa. 24:8; Ezek. 26:13).

The angel tells why Babylon has been cast down (18:23b-24): (1) because her merchants wantonly exalted themselves; (2) because by her sorceries, i.e., the wine of her impure passion, 18:3; 14:8, she has deceived all nations; and (3) finally, because she has spilled "the blood of prophets and of saints" (18:24; cf. Matt. 23:35). Small wonder the saints rejoiced so greatly at the downfall of this city and the kingdom of Antichrist (see 19:1-7).

F. Thanksgiving for the Fall of Babylon and the Marriage Supper of the Lamb (19:1-10)

1. Thanksgiving for the Fall of Babylon (19:1-5). In response to the cry "Rejoice over her, O heaven" (18:20), John tells of the jubilant Hallelujahs that the angelic multitude in heaven raises to God (19:1; cf. 5:9 ff.; 7:16 ff.; 11:15 ff.; 15:3; 16:5 ff.). This song of praise that they sing is not merely one which rejoices over the fall of Babylon, but it looks with anticipation to the coming of the messianic kingdom as prefigured in the Marriage Supper of the Lamb (19:6-10).

The multitude sings "Hallelujah" because the "salvation and glory and power" which men have looked for is about to come from God (19:1), and they praise God because these things belong to him and can only come from him. The word Hallelujah is used only in 19:2, 4, and 6 in the New Testament. In Hebrew it means "praise the Lord" and we get it from the Greek, which is the transliteration of the Hebrew. It is found in the closing verses of Psalms 104, 105, 106. Our Christian hymns get their Hallelujahs from this passage (19:1-10).

God's "judgments are true and just" (19:2; 15:3; 16:7) in causing the kingdom of the great Harlot to fall because she corrupted the earth and martyred the saints, and for this God "has avenged on her the blood of his servants," *lit.* "has exacted in vengeance the blood" (19:2b; cf. 6:10; Deut. 32:43).

As an unending cloud of smoke ascends from the city, the angelic host cries Hallelujah. The smoke arising to the accompaniment of the song is proof that Babylon has fallen (19:3; cf. 18:9; 14:11; Isa. 34:10).

Following the lead of the angelic host, "the twenty-four elders and the four living creatures" which surround the throne of God fell down before God saying, "Amen. Hallelujah!" (19:4; cf. 4:4 ff.; 5:8, 14; 11:16). The voice that calls from the throne to those upon earth is generally understood to be one of the four living creatures, since neither Christ nor God would call men to "praise *our* God." Note that the call is not limited to the martyrs, instead it calls for *all* God's servants, both the "small and great," to praise him (19:5; cf. Ps. 113:1; 134:1).

2. The Marriage Supper of the Lamb (19:6-10). In contrast to the awful fate awaiting Antichrist and his followers, the Lord grants John a vision of the impending, blessed, Messianic Age, which appears under the figure of "the marriage supper of the Lamb." Just as the fall of Babylon, Antichrist and his empire, are spoken of as already fallen, so this prophetic vision hails the kingdom as if already realized.

The singers here are in heaven, as suggested by the similes of the "many waters" and "mighty thunderpeals" (19:6; cf. 1:15; 6:1; 14:2). The angels cry Hallelujah because they see the Lord God Almighty as already reigning. "While God's supreme lordship over the universe is everywhere assumed in Hebrew and Christian thought, in a special eschatological sense he is said to *become king*, when his perfected kingdom shall have been established, and all opposing powers of evil destroyed; e.g., 11:15, 17; 12:10; Matt. 6:10; I Cor. 15:24" (Beckwith).

The cause for rejoicing in 19:7 is the marriage of the Lamb to his bride (19:7; cf. Matt. 5:12). The marriage of the Lamb, Christ, to his bride, the church, is a familiar figure or analogy in Biblical literature. In the Old Testament God is described as married to his people (cf. Hos. 2:19; Isa. 54:1-8; Ezek. 16:7). (In the apocryphal book of IV Ezra [9:1 ff.] Zion is portrayed as the bride of God.) In the New Testament our Lord Jesus used the figure of a marriage feast to illustrate the kingdom of heaven (Matt. 22:2 f.; 25:1 f.). But it is the Apostle Paul who explicitly refers to the church as the bride of Christ (II Cor. 11:2; Eph. 5:23 ff.); and it is the consummation of their marriage which John here presents as proleptically present (19:7-9; cf. 21:9 f.; 2:17 where the New Jerusalem is identified as the bride of Christ). The Lamb has come to claim his bride who has made herself ready, i.e., the church, the believing community, has been faithful to the testimony of Jesus. Unlike the diabolical character of the great Harlot, the bride of the Lamb is clothed in "fine linen, bright and pure." John tells us what the fine linen represents, namely, the *righteous deeds* of the saints" (19:8; 3:5; 6:11; cf. Phil. 2:12-13). Many scholars see in Romans (5:18) the antithesis to the "unrighteous acts" of the Antichrist (18:5).

The speaker addresses John and commands him to write the benediction of verse 9. Those invited are identical with the bride. Unlike those invited in the parable of the Wedding Feast in Matthew (22:14), the guests invited here all come. The voice gives "solemn assurance that the prophecies of John are "the words of God."

John, overwhelmed by the foregoing vision, falls prostrate before the "angel" (19:10). But the angel protests, telling John that he is a "fellow servant" of the Lord, along with him (John) and others who "hold fast to the testimony of (borne by) Jesus." He commands John to worship God. Many see here "a protest against an incipient angel worship which crept into the early church (cf. 22:8; Col. 2:18; Heb. 2:5).

John concludes this vision with the profound statement that "the testimony of Jesus is the spirit of prophecy." "Here John . . . joins hands with all the prophets to proclaim that Jesus' testimony to God — his complete revelation of God — is the very spirit and heart of the entire message of God's Word" (Love).

XI. THE CONQUEST OF EVIL AND THE CONSUMMA-TION OF THE KINGDOM (19:11–21:8)

We now come to the climax of the struggle to which the preceding chapters have looked forward with great anticipation — the defeat of the Antichrist and his forces.

A. The Fifth Horseman — Christ the Conqueror (19:11-16)

Again the veil into the heavens is drawn, and John sees the Christ seated upon a "white horse," and following him are the "armies of heaven" (19:11, 14). The Christ has come to do battle with the Beast and the False Prophet who are at Armageddon (cf. 16:13-16 and 19:19). The "white horse" of Christ symbolizes the victory anticipated (cf. 6:2). The title of Christ is "Faithful and True," titles which testify to the ideal character of the Messiah with which we are already familiar (19:11; cf. 1:5; 3:7, 14). He has come to execute "righteous" judgment and to make war against the Antichrist and his allies (cf. Isa. 11:3-5).

The character of Christ is now described (19:12-13). Note the "many diadems" which are appropriate for one who is "King of kings and Lord of lords" (19:12, 16). The secret name which no one knows cannot be any of those listed here (19:11-16). Some have thought it *Kyrios*, the Lord, because of Philippians 2:9-11 (cf. Acts 4:7, 12). Some have suggested that the name and its meaning will be shared with the saints in the New Age.

Verse 13 refers to "a robe dipped in blood." Most interpreters believe the primary reference is to the blood of his enemies who will be slain in the battle — a proleptic reference (cf. Isa. 63:1, 3) but this does not exclude a secondary reference "to the fact that this Conqueror overcame by the shedding of his own blood."

Another name by which the Christ is called is "The Word of God," a title which definitely links the thought of the Apocalypse with the prologue of the Fourth Gospel (19:13; cf. John 1:1-18).

Those who follow Christ into battle are not the saints, although they may be spectators (17:14), but angelic beings (19:14; cf. 12:7; 14:14-20). The "fine linen, *white* and *pure*," and the "white horses" symbolize the victory soon to be won.

Note that the enemy is not defeated by force of arms, but by the "sharp sword" which issues from his mouth. This points to the symbolic nature of the picture presented. There are numerous references to the conquest of the forces of evil by the "word of his mouth" — see especially 1:16; 2:12; Isaiah 11:4; Song of Sol. 17:27; Heb. 4:12). The nations which are smitten are those which are hostile to Christ, and *he* (emphatic) shall rule them with a "rod of iron" (19:15, 19-21; Isa. 14:4; Ps. 2:9). The messianic prophecy long foretold by the Psalmist (2:9) is now to be fulfilled. John says that Christ will tread the "wine press of the fury of the wrath of God the Almighty" and thereby press out the "wine" for the cup of God's wrath which the wicked must drink (19:15; cf. Isa. 63:3; 19:19-20; Rev. 14:10; 16:19).

Not only is Christ called the "Faithful and True," "The Word of God," but also the "King of kings and Lord of lords." The titles ascribed to God the Father are here applied to the son (cf. I Tim. 6:15).

B. The Conquest of the Beast and the False Prophet by the Messiah (19:17-21)

As the opposing forces are poised for mortal combat, John sees an angel "standing in the sun," i.e., in mid-heaven, and the angel calls to all the birds to come to the great feast which God is preparing for them. The background for this great feast is Ezekiel 39:17-20, only there it comes after the Messianic age, after the battle of Gog of the land of Magog, whereas here in Revelation it precedes the Messianic age (cf. Isa. 25:6; Luke 14:15 ff.; 22:30 f. where the idea of the banquet is associated with the coming of the messianic kingdom). Note the tragic contrast between the Marriage Supper of the Lamb and this "great supper" (19:6-10, 17-18).

The Beast and the kings of the earth, together with their armies, gather for battle against the Messiah at Armageddon (cf. 16:12-16; 17:13-14). Actually there is no battle; instead the Beast, Antichrist, and his agent the False Prophet, are captured and thrown into *the lake of fire* that burns with brimstone" (19:19-20). Beckwith calls attention to the fact that the fate of the Beast is different elsewhere. For example, I Thessalonians 2:8 says "he is slain by the breath of the Lord"; in the Apocalypse of Baruch 40:1-2, "he is bound and brought before the Messiah, who puts him to death"; in the Sibylline Oracles III 73 "he is burnt up." The "False Prophet" is described here in terms which make it clear that he is the same as the "second beast" or the "land Beast" of 13:11-17. The use of the expression "the lake of fire" to symbolize the place of punishment is peculiar to Revelation in the New Testament (19:20; cf. 20:10, 14-15; 21:8). Elsewhere in the New Testament expressions like "the valley of

Gehenna" or "Hinnom," "The unquenchable fire," "the hell [Gehenna] of fire," or "the furnace of fire" symbolizes the place of punishment (cf. Mark 9:43; Matt. 19:9; 18:42, 50; 10:28; Luke 12:5).

After the Beast and the False Prophet are cast into "the lake of fire," those who were deceived by the False Prophet and "received the mark of the Beast" and "worshiped its image" are "slain by the sword . . . that issues from his [Christ's] mouth" (19:21). Almost all interpreters understand the apocalyptic symbolism here to refer, not to a literal battle, but to the victory of Christ over the Antichrist and his forces. Beasley-Murray says the symbolism "is wholly judicial." Once the enemies of the Christ have been overcome, then the "great supper" takes place (19:17-18, 21b).

C. The Binding of Satan (20:1-3)

At last we come to that moment in history to which everything in this prophecy has been pointing, namely, the complete conquest of Satan himself. Although Satan's two agents have already been cast into "the lake of fire," Satan was still free to work his wiles. As long as he was free neither the Millennial Kingdom nor the New Heaven or Earth could become a reality. It was with profound gratitude and rejoicing, therefore, that John received the vision of the binding of Satan.

It is interesting that it is *an angel* who has the key to the bottomless pit and the great chain *and not* Christ. The "bottomless pit" or "abyss" is not the lake of fire, i.e., not the place of the final judgment (20:1; cf. 9:1; 17:8). The duration of the Dragon's captivity is to last "a thousand years" (20:2). John identifies the Dragon with the serpent, and clearly states that he is none other than the Devil and Satan. The "serpent" title reminds us of him who tempted Adam and Eve in Paradise, and all "the sons of Adam" since. But now that he is bound he will tempt man no more (20:2; cf. Gen. 3:1 ff.). The "Devil" is the New Testament name for the "Evil One" (Matt. 4:1; etc.). The Satan, "the accuser," is the title used in prophetic literature and elsewhere (Zech. 3:1-2; Job 1:6; Ps. 109:6; cf. I Tim. 3:11 with 3:6).

The idea of Satan being bound is a familiar one in the early Jewish literature (Tobit 8:3; I Enoch 10:4, 11-12; 88:1-3; Jubilies 23:29; Testament of Levi 18:21). Many interpret the millennium symbolically as referring to a specific period of time. Most modern scholars agree that there is no sound exegetical basis for spiritualizing the idea of the millennium as referring to the present church age as Augustine did. This "spiritualized" interpretation which does violence to the actual text of the Apocalypse did not come into the church until after Christianity was recognized as the "state" religion. Prior to this, Chapter twenty was almost always interpreted in a premillennial fashion. The church eagerly looked for Christ to return and "set up his kingdom" (cf. Acts 1:7). Satan is "sealed" in the pit so that he will not be able to deceive the nations as he had in the past, or will do when released after the thousand year period (20:3). "He must be loosed" — the release of Satan after the millennial reign of Christ is all in the plan of God (20:3b).

D. The Millennial Kingdom (20:4-6)

Just who are those who are seated on the "thrones," to whom judgment is committed? Some suggest that the "apostles" are intended (Matt. 19:28), while others take the reference to designate the "saints" (cf. Dan 7:9, 22, 26; I Cor. 6:2-3). This group seems to be different from those mentioned in the last half of verse 4.

In the Millennial Kingdom are those who: (1) were martyred, "beheaded," for their "testimony to Jesus and for the word of God" (cf. 1:9; 12:17; 19:10), and (2) those "who had not worshiped the beast or its image and had not received its mark on their foreheads or their hands" (20:4b). Many interpreters insist that only the martyred saints will come to life and "reign with Christ a thousand years" (20:4c). Beasley-Murray, and many others, however, maintain that the second group includes those who are alive at Christ's coming when the Millennial Age is inaugurated (cf. I Cor. 15:51-52). He believes that since the "Bride of the Lamb" symbolizes the entire church, it is natural to expect not only martyrs but *all the saints* to share in the millennial kingdom.

This "coming to life" John says is "the first resurrection" i.e., resurrection to share in the millennial kingdom (20:5). Again we should note that most scholars agree that there is no justification for interpreting this "first resurrection" in a spiritual sense as referring to the "new birth." Surely John would have made this point clear if this is what he had in mind! The rest of the dead are not resurrected — do not "come to life" — until the millennial reign is completed.

It needs to be emphasized that although the Apocalypse is the only New Testament book which clearly refers to the millennial reign of Christ, it is by no means a new idea in Hebrew-Christian thought. The prophets of the Old Testament looked forward with great anticipation to a messianic age here on earth, and John knew this well (cf. Isa. 2:1-4; 11:6-9; etc.). Later, Jewish thought was broadened to include not only a messianic age on earth, but because Apocalyptic writers especially believed that this world was intrinsically evil, they looked forward to an eternal age in the heavens or a spiritual existence. John reflects this two phased hope of a messianic age on earth and an eternal age in glory (cf. especially Ezek. 36—39 where a similar sequence is suggested, i.e., messianic era of peace, battle of Gog of the land of Magog, followed by a New Age).

Another passage which is often associated with the concept of a millennial reign of Christ, although it is not explicit, is I Corinthians 15:23-24, and with this is usually associated Philippians 3:21; I Thessalonians 4:14-17; Luke 14:14, and others.

Likewise, there are other references to the millennial age of a fixed duration in other Hebrew-Christian writings. IV Ezra 7:28-32 anticipates a messianic age of 400 years, whereas II Enoch 33:2 and the Epistle of Barnabas 15:2-8 support our Christian Apocalypse in anticipating a messianic reign of a thousand years. The idea of a thousand-year messianic age may be based upon Genesis 1 and Psalm 90:4, i.e., six millenniums of work followed by one of rest. The important thing to keep in mind is that the round number "a thousand" symbolizes something complete. Satan is completely bound and the saints enter upon an era of "perfect and glorious victory" (Milligan).

Verse 6 rightly says that those who do endure to the end — even suffering martyrdom if need be — will share in the first resurrection, and they will indeed be reckoned as "blessed" and "holy" (20:6a). The "second death" which will follow "the great white throne judgment" will not affect those who have been resurrected to reign with him a thousand years (20:6; cf. 20:14-15; 21:8; Matt. 10:28). John adds that those who are privileged to be with Christ in his millennial kingdom will serve him in some capacity — "They shall be priests of God and of Christ."

E. The Loosing of Satan and God's Final Conquest (20:7-10)

Now at God's bidding, for John believes God is in absolute control of all things, "Satan will be loosed from his prison" and he will go forth "to deceive the nations which are at the four corners of the earth" (20:7). These nations are identified with Gog and Magog, whom Ezekiel reckoned as the diabolical leader of the forces of evil. In Ezekiel (38—39), however, Gog seems to be the prince, or ruler, and Magog seems to be the land over which he rules. But in later Jewish apocryphal literature, including the recently discovered *Qumran Scroll*, "The War of the Sons of Light Against the Sons of Darkness," both names seem to represent peoples. C. Anderson Scott says that "in later apocalyptic literature they are conventional symbols for the world hostile to Israel or the people of God." Here in Revelation they definitely seem to symbolize those nations deceived by, and in league with, Satan.

This innumerable host will surround "the camp of the saints and the beloved city," but true to the faith of John, God intervenes on behalf of his people and he sends fire down from heaven to consume them (20:8-9; cf. Ezek. 38:22; 39:6; Gen. 19:24). "The camp of the saints" and "the beloved city" signify the same thing, namely Jerusalem (cf. Ps. 77:68; 87:2). Jerusalem is called "the beloved city" because that is where Christ reigns.

The Devil or Satan, however, is not consumed by the fire; instead, he is seized and thrown into "the lake of fire" where the Beast and the False Prophet have already been cast, and there all three, "the trinity of evil," are "tormented day and night for ever and ever" (20:10; cf. 19:20).

F. The General Resurrection and the Last Judgment (20:11-15)

After the vision in which the Devil is thrown into the lake of fire, John sees God seated upon "a great white throne" ready to judge *all men* (20:11; cf. Isa. 6:1; Dan. 7:8).

The "throne" is great in comparison to those in 20:4, and is "white," symbolizing "the intensity of Divine purity." John actually does not mention God's name, but speaks as a Hebrew using the periphrasis instead of his name — "him who sat upon it" (cf. Dan. 7:10; also IV Ezra 7:33). God is usually the judge in Revelation, except in 22:12 where Christ speaks of coming with judgment. From the presence of God upon his throne the "earth and sky fled away" (20:11b; cf. 12:20; Isa. 61:6). Cf. II Peter 3:10-12 which says that "the heavens will be *kindled* and *dissolved*, and the elements will melt with fire."

Before the throne of judgment are brought the dead, "both small and great" (20:12a). Evidently the "souls" are now clothed in a "body." The basis of judgment is twofold, namely the "books" in which man's deeds are recorded and the "book of life" (20:12). The idea of "books of judgment" is a familiar one in the Old Testament and in Jewish literature (cf. Dan. 7:10; Mal. 3:16; IV Ezra 6:20; I Enoch 90:22). It is most important to grasp the significance of this double check. As our Lord Jesus said, "Not everyone that says to me, 'Lord, Lord,' shall enter the kingdom of heaven, but he who *does* the will of my Father who is in heaven" (Matt. 7:21; cf. 7:24 ff.; 25:31-46; II Cor. 5:10). The "book of life" contains the names of the redeemed (cf. 3:5; 13:8; Luke 10:20; Phil. 4:3).

Verse 13 makes it clear that *all men* are to be judged on that day. Not only will those who died on earth be resurrected, but also those who so tragically died at sea. "Hades" seems to refer to the abode of the wicked, although in earlier Jewish thought it was the abode of both the righteous and the wicked (IV Ezra 7:32; I Enoch 61:5, etc.).

After the judgment those whose names were not found in the book of life are thrown into the "lake of fire," which is the second death (20:14-15; cf. 20:6; 2:11; 21:8; Matt. 25:41). But even more important to the believer is the good news that God will cast both "death and hades," which seem to be personified here as two demons, into the lake of fire (20:14; cf. I Cor. 15:26, 54).

G. The New Creation (21:1-8)

With the "last judgment" completed, John now is granted a vision of the blessed eternal kingdom of God, in which the true church is united with her God and Savior. The "secular world," i.e., the world organized against God, has been overthrown, and God now ushers in the new creation as the eternal dwelling place for his faithful ones. Some interpreters see in 21:1-5 "an anticipative and concise" picture of the new heaven and the new earth and an amplification of this in a detailed description of the glorified church and her union with God and the Lamb in 20:9—22:5. It seems, however, that Kelly, Zalin, Charles, and Beasley-Murray have assessed the problem more accurately by seeing 20:9—22:5 as describing the characteristics of life in the millennial kingdom 20:4-6. Beasley-Murray offers the following reasons for the above division: (1) 21:24-27 describes the conditions which one would naturally associate with the continuation of the earthly city — "nations" walk in the light of the city, "kings of the earth shall bring their glory into it," and the wicked and unclean are excluded from it; (2) 22:2 refers to the leaves of the tree of life being used for "the healings of the nations" — a statement that is more intelligible if applied to the earthly city; (3) in 22:12-15 Christ pronounces a blessing upon those saints who are still living and they are encouraged to be faithful to the end, and he issues a warning to the wicked that they shall be excluded. Admittedly, both interpretations of 21—22 have their difficulties, but the above seems to have the least.

John's vision of "a new heaven and a new earth" is in harmony with the great expectations of the prophets and other Jewish writers (21:1; cf. Isa. 65:17 ff.; 66:22; Hos. 2:18; Ps. 102:25-26; Matt. 5:18; Mark 13:31; Luke 6:17; II Peter 3:12; I Enoch 91:26). This present world is not good enough for the eternal kingdom, therefore, the first order must pass away before a new one can be ushered in. The "sea" has no place in the new creation because to the ancients the sea "was only turbulent, estranging, hostile; it devoured men with its insatiable maw." Some see here reference to "the primitive oriental myth of the Creator's conflict with a sea-monster, such as appears in the allusions to the dragon, Rahab and Leviathan (cf. Isa. 27:1; 51:9; Job 26:13), but there is no such intimation made by John" (Beckwith).

Into this new world John sees "the holy city, *new Jerusalem*, coming down out of heaven from God" (21:2; cf. 3:12). This is a *new* Jerusalem created by God and given by him, *not* one "renovated" by social reform, etc. Other New Testament passages parallel this idea; Galatians 4:25; Philippians 3:20; Hebrews 12:22; cf. also the Apocalypse of Baruch 4:1 ff., and IV Ezra 10:1 ff. The city is described as "a bride adorned for her husband," and thereby is identified with the church — the body of believers (21:2b; cf. 19:609; Matt. 22:2 ff.; Isa. 61:10—62:5).

The "great voice" proclaims that God once more dwells with men (21:3). While it is true that God is with us in Christ now — Emmanuel, the promise contained in the name Emmanuel will be perfectly fulfilled on *that day* (cf. Matt. 1:23; Jer. 24:7; Ezek. 11:20; 48:35). There is nothing between the child and his Father now (cf. I John 1:1-3; I Cor. 13:12). The word "dwelling" is the one used in the Septuagint for the tabernacle in the wilderness (cf. Heb. 8:2; 9:11; John 1:14).

"He will *dwell* with them." John uses the same verb here that he uses in his Gospel (1:14). The dwelling place of God among his chosen people, symbolized by the tabernacle and the shekinah, will be with men, apart from any visible temple (cf. Lev. 26:11-12; Ezek. 37:27; Zech. 8:8; Jer. 31:33). Turner suggests that, if we read "peoples," as some Greek manuscripts do, there is a reference to the breaking down of national barriers (21:3; cf. John 10:16).

The quality of life in the new eternal order described in verses 3 and 4 suggest the idea that the complete fellowship broken by the fall is now restored (cf. Gen. 2:15-22; 3:8). The promises of 21:4 reflect the thought of numerous other passages from the Old and New Testaments. For the "tears" being wiped away, see 7:17; Isaiah 25:8; for the abolition of "death," see Isaiah 25:8; I Corinthians 15:54; for the absence of "mourning," "crying" and "pain," see Isaiah 35:10; 65:16-19. All these things, the things which characterized life in the old aeon or order, have now passed away.

God now speaks to John in words that closely parallel those of the Apostle Paul, "Behold, I make all things new" (21:5; cf. II Cor. 5:17; Isa. 43:19; Jer. 31:22). The "new Jerusalem" is only for those who have already experienced the "new life" in Christ — for those who have *already* "tasted the goodness of the word of God and the powers of the age to come" (Heb. 6:5).

The Lord God tells John to "write this," i.e., the revelation contained in 21:1-5, for the revelation is "trustworthy and true." The last phrase would be better translated "faithful and true" in keeping with John's practice elsewhere in the Apocalypse (3:14; 19:11; cf. also 22:6).

With the words *It is done* God now confirms the fact that his redemptive task is complete. Through the "seed of woman," Jesus the Christ, the Serpent and his seed have been destroyed (21:6; cf. Gen. 3:15). The "It is done" of judgment has given way to the "It is done" of redemption (cf. 16:17 with 21:6). This was accomplished by none other than Almighty God, "The Alpha and Omega, the beginning and the end" (21:6; 1:8). To all who thirst in their souls for true spiritual satisfaction, God promises to give them water freely "from the fountain of the water of life." This promise, partially realized in Christ while on earth, is fully realized in his eternal kingdom (cf. Isa. 55:1; John 4:13; 7:37; Rev. 22:17; with 22:6; 7:17).

Those who resist the temptation to deny the Christ and remain true to the end, i.e., "he who conquers," "will be rewarded with the relation of perfect sonship with God" (cf. Gal. 4:7; I John 3:2).

But to "the cowardly, the faithless, the polluted" (i.e., primarily the Christians who corrupt themselves by worshiping the Beast rather than endure persecution, and the pagans who practice the familiar vices murder, fornication, sorcery, idolatry and lying) there awaits nothing but the terrible "second death" (21:8). The torment of the second death is symbolized by the familiar imagery of the "lake that burns with fire and brimstone" (cf. Gen. 19:24; Ps. 11:6; Isa. 30:33; Ezek. 38:22; Rev. 14:10; 19-20).

XII. A DETAILED DESCRIPTION OF THE NEW JERUSA-
LEM (21:9—22:5)

As stated earlier these verses probably are intended as a description of Jerusalem in the millennial kingdom, although many scholars believe it describes the eternal kingdom. The prophetic books which form the background for John's description are primarily Isaiah and Ezekiel, as we shall see.

A. The Measuring of the City (21:9-17)

The angel who comes to show John the "Bride, the wife of the Lamb" is one of the angels associated with "the seven bowls full of the seven last plagues" (21:9; cf. 17:1). It seems obvious that the close parallelism in language between 21:9-10 and 17:1, 3 suggests that John is contrasting the new Jerusalem with the Harlot city, and the Bride with the Harlot Beast.

As Ezekiel the prophet was taken up into a "very high mountain," so John is carried by the Spirit to a "high mountain" from which he is shown "the holy city Jerusalem coming down out of heaven from God" (22:10; cf. Ezek. 40:2 ff.). The city is lighted, not by the sun or moon, but by "the glory of God" (22:11, 23; cf. Isa. 61:1; Ezek. 43:2, 4-5). The radiance of the city is like a "jasper," clear as crystal, perhaps a diamond.

The structure of the city is similar to that found in Ezekiel's description (44:31 ff.). The city is walled to keep out the wicked (cf. 21:27; 22:14-15). Each of the four walls has "three gates" with an angel at each gate, and the name of one of the tribes inscribed on each (21:12-13). For the "angels" see Isaiah 62:6 and I Chronicles 8:14. The perfect city is one which has "watchmen." To convey the Christian conviction that the church of God is one, the angel reveals to John that there are twelve foundation stones under the four walls on which are inscribed the "names of the twelve apostles of the Lamb" (22: 14). The "patriarchs" and the "apostles" are the foundation of the church (cf. Eph. 2:20). Most interpreters agree that the twelve apostles is a *corporate figure* symbolizing the new Israel of God, even as the twelve patriarchs symbolize the old Israel, therefore, it is fruitless to speculate about whether John included himself or whether Paul is included. As C. Anderson Scott says: "The Twelve . . . are here referred to in a corporate and official capacity, and any attempt to individualize them is quite out of place."

Whereas in Ezekiel the angel has a "measuring reed" in his hand, here the angel has "a measuring rod of gold" with which he is to lay out the dimensions of the city (21:15; cf. Ezek. 40:3). The city is perfectly square, a perfect cube (I Kings 6:20). Most interpreters agree that the symbolism behind this picture is the "holy of holies." The dimensions of the city which "lies four square" and its walls, are both multiples of twelve, the church number. Beckwith says that "the Apocalyptist . . . is struggling to express by symbols the vastness, the perfect symmetry, and the splendor of the new Jerusalem. Perhaps the great height of the city figures the blending of heaven and earth. . . ."

B. The Appearance and Character of the City (21:18-27)

The main idea John is seeking to convey to his readers is that the city is ideally perfect. The precious stones which adorn the "foundations of the wall" are almost all found in the breastplate of the high priest (21:19:20; cf. Exod. 28:17 ff.; 39:10 ff.) and in the description of Tyre by Ezekiel (28:13; cf. Isa. 54:11-12), although some of the identifications are doubtful and impossible.

For the background for the gates made of "a single pearl" Beckwith cites an interesting quotation from the Talmud. He quotes from Wetstein who cites a passage from the *Talmud* (*Baba batha*, 75, 1): "God will bring gems and pearls thirty cubits long and wide, and will hollow these out to the height of twenty cubits and to the breadth of ten cubits, and place them in the gates of Jerusalem."

In the city there is no need for a temple, for "the Lord God the Almighty and the Lamb" will be there (21:22). John began his prophecy with the worship of God and the Lamb and he ends it in the same way. Again, the fact that God communes directly with man suggests that Paradise is restored. Redeemed man worships in "spirit and in truth" (cf. John 4:21).

Verse 23 is thoroughly Johannine in thought. The statement that "the glory of God is its light" reminds us of I John 1:5, and the expression "the lamp is the Lamb" reminds us of our Lord's words, "I am the light of the world" in John 8:12 (cf. 1:9; II Cor. 4:6; Heb. 1:3). With the light of God in the city, there is no need for the sun or moon. The concept of the shekinah glory of God is definitely intended here (cf. 21:3).

The thought of 21:24-26 reflects Isaiah 60:1-11. John is seeking to convey here the universal sway of Jehovah God. Kings and nations shall walk in the light of Jehovah, and bring their glory to the city (cf. Isa. 60:3, 5; 2:3; Ps. 72:10). The fact that the "gates" are never shut, and that there is "no night there," assures the saints that in the millennial kingdom there is nothing to fear. The only ones admitted into the city will be those whose names "are written in the Lamb's book of life" (21:27; 3:5; 13:8; 20:12).

C. The River of the Water of Life and the Tree of Life (22:1-5)

Flowing from "the throne of God and the Lamb" is "the *river of the water of life*" (22:1-2a). The idea of a river in the restored Paradise comes from the description of the Garden of Eden (Gen. 2:10). Elsewhere in Scripture "waters," and "living waters" are used to symbolize the blessings which flow to man from the presence of God (cf. Jer. 2:13; Ezek. 47:1-12; Ps. 46:4; see also John 4:10; Rev. 7:7; 21:6). Whereas in Ezekiel the streams flow from the restored temple, in John's vision the stream issues from the throne.

Although "the tree of life" is in the singular, the context of the verse indicates that "tree" should be understood generically. "The tree of life" cannot be on "either side of the river" if there is only one. In the Garden of Eden (Gen. 2:9) there was only one tree, but in the new Paradise, there are many trees which will yield fruit, "the leaves of these trees" serving to heal the nations (22:2; cf. Ezek. 47:12). The flaming sword which once barred man's approach to the tree has been removed, so that the saints might partake freely (cf. Gen. 3:22-24).

"There shall no more be anything accursed" (22:3; cf. Zech. 14:14), because anything accursed is a barrier between God and man. In the millennial kingdom and the new creation nothing that breaks man's fellowship with God will exist. Since sin is removed, "the throne of God and of the Lamb" can dwell there. John makes it clear that the throne of God and the throne of the Lamb are identical (22:3; cf. 3:2; 7:17; John 14:23).

"His servants shall worship him." What John is saying is that in the kingdom his servants, or bond-servants (*douloi*), will render God not "worship" but *lit.* "the service of ministry," (*latreuō*). It should be encouraging to know that in the kingdom the saints do not sit around playing harps but have a chance to continue in the service of God.

"They shall see his face" (22:4a). The beatific vision which had been denied men (Exod. 38:20) becomes the reward of the faithful in the kingdom (cf. Ps. 17:15; Matt. 5:8; I John 3:2; I Cor. 13:12). On the foreheads of the faithful shall be written

108

"his name," i.e., the name of God and the Lamb (22:4; cf. 14:1; 7:3).

The saints shall reign with God and the Lamb "for ever and ever" (22:5). This verse apparently refers to the eternal kingdom and not the millennium. The thought of "the saints of the Most High," or "the people of the saints of the Most High," is derived from Daniel 7:18, 27.

XIII. THE EPILOGUE (22:6-21)

A. The Revelation Confirmed (22:6-9)

It is difficult to know exactly who is speaking in the various parts of this epilogue, but as Beasley-Murray concludes: "In the last resort it matters little; the speaker is ultimately Christ, whose messenger the angel is (9), and whose utterances John records as a prophet."

Christ seems to be speaking here and confirming the revelation given in the Apocalypse — "these words are faithful [trustworthy] and true" (22:6a; cf. 21:5).

"The Lord, the God of the spirits of the prophets." The meaning is clarified by 19:10 where "the spirit of prophecy" is the Spirit of God active in inspiring prophecy. What seems to be meant above is that the spirits of the prophets are inspired (cf. I Cor. 14:32). As is customary in apocalyptic, the revelation is mediated through an angel. The message revealed, namely, the Apocalypse, is one that "must soon take place."

"I am coming soon," uttered by our Lord Jesus, is one of the themes of the epilogue and the book — it is the blessed hope of the church (22:7a; cf. 2:5, 16; 3:11; 16:15; 22:12). In the light of his soon return, John (?) announces that a special blessing is in store for the one who "keeps", i.e., heeds, "the words of the *prophecy* of this book" (22:7b). Note how John subordinates his apostolic rule to his prophetic mission.

Verses 8 and 9 are interpreted by some as being a polemic against the worship of angelic beings, a form of idolatry which evidently troubled the early church (cf. Col. 2:18). Probably the real import of these two verses, however, is to emphasize the *prophetic* rank of the author — "I am a fellow servant with you and your brethren the prophets."

B. Warnings and Promises (22:10-15)

Unlike the advice given to Daniel (12:4) and to John earlier (10:4), John is now counseled not to seal up his prophecy because "the time is near," i.e., the return of Christ (22:10; cf. 19:11-21).

"Let the evildoer still do evil" (22:11). There seems to be a note of irony here. Because the time is so short, "no change in the wicked is to be looked for, let him continue in his wickedness, if he will; his penalty will soon fall" (Beckwith). "The righteous" and "the holy," however, are urged to continue to be steadfast in the faith, because the end is at hand.

In words that echo those of Isaiah (40:10; 62:11), the Lord announces that he will soon come "to repay everyone for what he has done" (22:12; cf. 2:23; Rom. 2:26; Ps. 62:12).

In verse 13 the qualities of God are claimed by Jesus, and it will be as "the Eternal One" that he will judge and reward.

The last beatitude is directed to those who have washed their robes in the blood of the Lamb (22:14; cf. 3:4; 7:14; I Cor. 6:11). These have "the right to the tree of life," *lit.* "power over," i.e., the liberty to eat of the fruit. The "gates" of the city open to the righteous, but all those who practice evil are shut out. "Dogs" denotes base and malicious persons (22:15; cf. Phil. 3:2; Ps. 22:16, 20; II Kings 8:13). Dog was the term the Jews used to designate the heathen or Gentiles (Matt. 7:16; 15:26). "Sorcerers" probably designated "the whole class of necromancers and dealers in magic who flourished so greatly at this period." It is interesting to note that the one who practices "lies" is at the end of the list (cf. 22:15 with 21:8, 27).

C. The Witness of Christ and the Prophet to the Visions (22:16-20)

Now Jesus himself steps forward to authenticate the angel's testimony to John. The message is addressed to "the churches" (22:16; cf. 1:4, 20; 2:1 ff.). Jesus identifies himself as "the root and the offspring of David" (5:5; cf. Isa. 11:1, 10; Matt. 1:1; 22:42), and "the bright morning star" (cf. Num. 24:17; Rev. 2:28; II Peter 1:19).

The invitation to "Come" is best taken, not as an appeal to Christ for his return, but as an evangelistic appeal to sinners to repent and acknowledge Christ as Lord. The marriage of the Lamb is still in the future (22:17; cf. 19:7). The "Spirit" is probably the Spirit of Christ speaking through John. The "bride" is the church who joins with Christ in calling men to repentance. The one who "hears" is not the one who hears the Apocalypse read, but the one who hears and is converted and then joins in inviting others to "come" to Christ. The one who is "thirsty" is invited to "take the *water of life*" freely, without price (cf. Isa. 55:1).

Verses 18 and 19 constitute a warning to any who might read or hear this book read. A similar warning is found in Deuteronomy 4:2; 12:32. The teachings of this book are not to be picked over as one picks and chooses food in a cafeteria, the entire message is to be taken seriously. To "add" or to "take away" from the teachings of this book, is to forfeit one's share in the kingdom as described in 22:14.

The Lord Jesus, who testifies to the message of the Apocalypse, says, "Surely, I am coming soon" (22:20). This is the motif of the entire book. It is the only hope of salvation for the church. To this clear promise of Jesus, John cries, "Amen, i.e., "so be it," and then he prays the ejaculatory prayer of the early church, *Maranatha* (Aramaic) which means "Come, Lord! Jesus!"

D. Benediction (22:21)

John concludes his message with a benediction like those in other New Testament epistles, which probably suggests that the author intended that the church should read the Apocalypse in public worship services. His parting prayer for the suffering saints is that the all sufficient "grace" of Jesus Christ be with them all.